Diary of a
YPRES NUN
October 1914-May 1915

T0341655

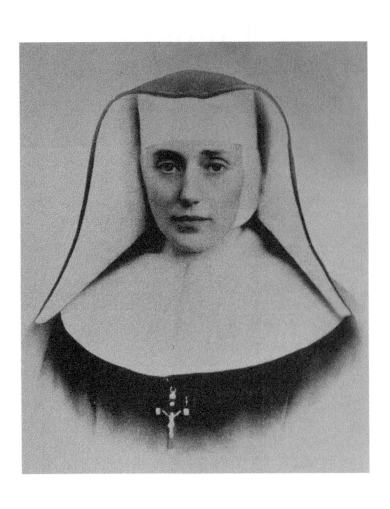

Diary of a
YPRES NUN
October 1914 - May 1915

The Diary of Soeur Marguerite
of the Sisters of Lamotte
*Suffering and Sacrifice
in the First World War*

Introduced and Edited by
Linda Palfreeman

sussex
ACADEMIC
PRESS
Brighton • Chicago • Toronto

2 4 6 8 10 9 7 5 3 1

First published in 2017 by
SUSSEX ACADEMIC PRESS
PO Box 139
Eastbourne BN24 9BP

Distributed in the United States of America by
SUSSEX ACADEMIC PRESS
Independent Publishers Group
814 N. Franklin Street, Chicago, IL 60610

British Library Cataloguing in Publication Data
A CIP catalogue record for this book is available from the British Library.

Library of Congress Cataloging-in-Publication Data
Names: Marguerite, Soeur, author. | Palfreeman, Linda, editor.
Title: Diary of a Ypres nun, October 1914–May 1915 : the diary of Soeur Marguerite of the Sisters of Lamotte : suffering and sacrifice in the First World War / introduced and edited by Linda Palfreeman.
Other titles: Diary of Soeur Marguerite of the Sisters of Lamotte
Description: Brighton ; Portland : Sussex Academic Press, 2017. | Includes bibliographical references.
Identifiers: LCCN 2017007149 | ISBN 9781845198701 (pbk : alk. paper)
Subjects: LCSH: Marguerite, Soeur—Diaries. | Ypres, 2nd Battle of, Ieper, Belgium, 1915. | Ypres, 1st Battle of, Ieper, Belgium, 1914. | World War, 1914–1918—Personal narratives. | World War, 1914–1918—Medical care. | World War, 1914–1918—Religious aspects—Catholic Church. | Friends Ambulance Unit.
Classification: LCC D542.Y7 M3313 2017 | DDC 940.4/75092—dc23
LC record available at https://lccn.loc.gov/2017007149

Typeset and designed by Sussex Academic Press, Brighton & Eastbourne.
Printed and bound by CPI Group (UK) Ltd, Croydon, CR0 4YY

CONTENTS

INTRODUCTION

The campaign in Flanders, with its several successive battles, would be the longest of the Great War and the costliest in terms of human life. At the centre of the fearful and prolonged barrages of shelling, by the military of both sides in the conflict, lay the town of Ypres – the previously tranquil town known largely for its splendid Cloth Hall and cathedral, its butter and its lace. That was, tragically, about to change, as Ypres was blasted, quite literally, to worldwide infamy as symbol of the suffering, sacrifice and destruction that inevitably results from war.

The images of immediate post-war Ypres, or rather, of the city's charred remains, will forever epitomise the horror and untold misery provoked by the First World War. And although today completely rebuilt, the city remains an everlasting memorial to those – both soldiers and civilians – who lived, fought and died there. Trenches and shell craters have been preserved for posterity, while uniforms, guns and ammunition, as well as more personal artefacts, are on public display, alongside records of some of the men to which such poignant memorabilia once sadly belonged. The most iconic and imposing symbol of all is the Menin Gate Memorial to the Missing which bears the names of 54,896 British and Empire soldiers who died in and around Ypres and have no known grave. Shortly after its inauguration, in 1927, the citizens of Ypres formed the Last Post Association to pay lasting tribute to all those who died in defence of their town and its people. Every evening, beneath Ieper's monumental Menin Gate, in fair weather or foul, normal everyday life comes to a stop. The soul-searching silence is pierced only by the sad strains of the bugle sounding the Last Post, in remembrance of the many thousands of dead – those who lie among the rows upon rows of graves now shrouding Flanders' fields, and those who remain eternally 'lost'. From the First Battle of Ypres to the end of the war, between 220,000 and 240,000 men from Britain and the Empire would die within the infamous Ypres Salient – roughly a third of all those who were killed in the First World War. When the war was finally over, this catastrophic loss of life would lead Winston

Churchill to declare of Ypres, that 'more sacred place for the British race does not exist in the world.'

But there is yet another story that remains to be told about life – and death – in Ypres during those dark days of conflict – a tragic drama played out largely beneath the town's battered ramparts, in the dismal underworld of passageways and cellars that for eight months provided shelter for the unfortunate townspeople trapped, centre-stage, in this abominable theatre of war. Here, too, the war discovered heroes – heroes who made it their mission to bring care, comfort and sustenance to those existing in fear and in desperate circumstances. These courageous and selfless individuals adminis- tered much-needed medical attention, distributed food and clothing, provided milk for babies and set up orphanages and schools for chil- dren. Where possible, they provided refugees with means of much-needed employment and, when the final moment came, when blackened embers and brick dust were all that remained of the pulverised town, they were there to evacuate the remaining inhabi- tants to places of safety.

These quiet heroes were members of the Friends Ambulance Unit, staffed chiefly by young men belonging to the Society of Friends (or Quakers) who had left Britain for France and Belgium with the inten- tion of giving medical assistance to sick and wounded soldiers at the front. (Their story of the ensuing events is told in the companion volume to the present work: *Friends in Flanders: The humanitarian aid of the Friends' Ambulance Unit during the First World War.*) The other unlikely heroes already formed an essential and inseparable part of the moral and social fibre of the beleaguered town: these were the local priest, Camille Delaere, and his faithful assistant, Soeur Marguerite of the Sisters of Lamotte. The solid bond of friendship and mutual respect that developed between these erstwhile strangers was shaped by a common aim, that of rescuing what they could of the miserable life remaining in Ypres after the outbreak of war – something of which the authorities appeared incapable or unwilling.

Historically, Ypres was no stranger to siege conditions. It had been (and, to some extent, still was) a prosperous town of rich medieval heritage, famous for its textile industry. The year 1260 saw the commencement of the construction of the *Lakenalle* or Cloth Hall – a magnificent trading centre, thought to be the largest secular building in Europe, a symbol of the town's wealth and importance. However, the ensuing 'Hundred Years' War' saw the textile trade suffer a gradual decline. Ypres was subject to subsequent periods of Spanish and French rule, during which time the town's fortifications were successively modified.[1] During the French occupation in the 1680s, this task was assumed by the French military engineer Sébastien Le Prestre, Seigneur de Vauban. Vauban remodelled the defences, adding sluice gates to divert water into the ditches around the city walls, to cause flooding. Thus, by the time Belgium finally gained independence in 1830, Ypres had become a strong fortress. Conscious of the fact that Belgium presented a prime strategic base of attack for any power wishing to invade Britain, the British Government negotiated the Treaty of London, guaranteeing Belgian neutrality. It was signed in 1839, by all the major European powers, only to be completely disregarded later, in 1914, by Germany, in its lust for war.

There had been no great industrialisation in Ypres. Some small factories continued to produce the cloths for which it had become famed and there were flourishing breweries using the locally-grown hops. Tobacco was also cultivated on a small scale and the fertile soil provided rich pasture for cattle – dairy produce, especially butter, being another renowned local commodity. Another of these was lace – lace-making providing employment for a large part of the female population of Ypres, as it did in many other towns in Flanders.

Eventually, in the late 19th century, the decision was made to demolish the fortifications of Ypres, which were thought to be restricting the growth of the town. The western sections of the ramparts were pulled down, but as the town showed no signs of subsequent growth (the population at the time numbered less than 19,000) the demolition was never completed – roughly half of the ramparts remaining intact, together with the maze of underground tunnels, passageways and casements that had been built into them. The casements that existed below the ramparts between the Menin Gate and the Lille Gate would provide excellent shelter, for both military and civilians, during the tremendous shelling to which Ypres would be subjected during the coming war. But that part of the story is best told by Soeur Marguerite . . .

LINDA PALFREEMAN

Overleaf

Chateau Elizabeth Hospital staff, Poperinghe 1915. Dr Rees, seated centre, is flanked by the Belgian countesses (© Religious Society of Friends (Quakers) in Britain).

Curé Delaere and sisters rescuing valuables (Cadbury Research Library: Special Collections, University of Birmingham).

NOTICE

This is not a literary work, it is a diary, in which a witness has noted, day by day, the events that took place from October 1914 to May 1915, in the dying city of Ypres.

This diary makes claim to only one thing – accuracy. The author has witnessed the events, and has narrated with painstaking care what happened within her sphere of daily activity, and her diary will make a valuable contribution to whoever writes 'The Last Days of Ypres'.

The reader will be amazed to learn what has been done, within this great charitable army, by a frail nun. And that astonishment will have turned to admiration by the time the reader closes the book after reading it.

ROUEN, 4 March 1918.

THE DIARY

THE DIARY

YPRES

Ypres is located SW of West Flanders, on the Ieperlee and [in 1914] had a population of 17,500.[2]

Ypres was famous for its lace, its cloth, its ribbons and butter for which there was a very large market. Every week, around 20,000 kilos were sold.

Ypres! It is said that the city took its name from a certain 'Hyperborus' who settled here in Roman times with 700 slaves, at the place now called Langemeersch. He built a castle for himself and surrounded it by huts that served as homes for his slaves, but soon he was attacked and beaten by other neighbouring nobles.

At the time of the *communes*, Ypres was one of the most important Flemish cities and rivaled Ghent and Bruges. The city was much larger than it is now and had more than 200,000 inhabitants whose main occupation was the manufacture of cloth. Ypres cloth had a worldwide reputation. The many great monuments of Ypres, including the Halles and Saint Martin Church occupy prime position, bearing witness to its past grandeur.

Les Halles included the Town Hall, Pauwels Hall and the Magistrates' Hall which were famous for their murals. They provided us with paintings showing the prosperity of the industries and occupations in the Middle Ages, and events in the history of Ypres, such as: the return of the people of Ypres after the Crusade; the visit of Margaret of Constantinople to the prison on a Good Friday; her visit to the civil hospital; a fête in les Halles; the plague in Ypres in the fifteenth century.

The Church of St. Martin contained, besides many remarkable paintings, the tomb of Jansen, bishop of Ypres who remains sadly infamous as the author of the heretic Jansenism.[3]

Two local festivals were celebrated annually in Ypres: one called Thuyndag a second named Kattefeest (the Festival of the Cat). If we are to believe tradition, it took its name from a curious old custom, which was to throw a cat from the belfry on the first Wednesday after the first week of Lent. The feast of Thuyndag celebrated the rescuing of the city that was being besieged by the English in 1383, a rescue brought about by the miraculous intervention of Notre Dame of Thuyne, patron saint of the city.

From 1559 to 1801 Ypres was the seat of a bishop.

EVENTS

On 7 October 1914 – the day of *Notre Dame des Victoires*, at about 11 o'clock in the morning, we heard rumbling cannon in the hamlet of Hooge. There must have been a battle engaged. After lunch, at about half past one, cannon fire was heard near the Lille Gate; the inhabitants of this area fled to the *Grand Place*. Two or three missiles fell on the *Sœurs Noires*[4] and Mr. Banckaert's house.

Our students, numbering over 400, were preparing to enter their respective classes, but in an instant all escaped through the school door, crying with fright.[5]

Eight or nine shrapnel bombs were dropped, and then all was silent. However, a few minutes later we saw some German soldiers heading from the *Grand Place* to the Lille Gate, from where they soon returned, followed by hundreds of cyclists. It was the same day that Mr. Henri Vandamme was killed by a bullet that passed through the window of his house while he was there with his six-year-old grand-daughter. Shrapnel bombs were dropped on the city in the area of Steenen Haan, chausée de Comines; one fell in rue de Cannon, but without causing damage; another went through a window on the first floor of No. 2 rue Grimminck and made an enormous hole in the back wall; a third fell on the Saint-Pierre church, but made only two small holes in the roof. It is amazing that no one was hit by the small lead balls that flew on all sides from exploding shrapnel bombs. Our infant school children amused themselves by picking up the bullets.

The Germans spent the night in the city and surrounding areas. Their number was estimated at about 20,000. They had with them a lot of munitions:1,200 machine guns, 600 guns, and 30 mobile kitchens, they say. It was also said that they were what remained of the army of Prince Heisel who had been beaten in Verdun and who had had 70,000 men. These looters did a fair amount of damage in the town, mostly attacking the goldsmiths, clothing and food shops.

These were German infantry and troops from the 4th cavalry corps. They were being deployed to the north of the town by the German Chief of Staff, General von Falkenhayn, with the intention of cutting off any French or British troops heading for the Flanders coast. (This was part of the so-called 'race to the sea'.) While the majority of troops went on to Hazebrouck, some hundred-or-so men remained in Ypres overnight on 7 October, to rest their horses and to await orders. Demanding freedom of the city, German officers took the entire contents of the town's coffers (some 65,000 francs) and the little that there was of value in the Post Office. The mayor, Mr Colaert, appealed to citizens to stay calm, while soldiers flooded the shops, mostly in search of food. Rarely did they pay for what they took – including clothing and jewellery. Hay and oats for the horses were also requisitioned and bakers were ordered to bake thousands of loaves of bread for the following morning. Meanwhile, soldiers were billeted, for the night, in public buildings, schools, in army barracks and in private homes. Though historians note no vindictive destruction or atrocity on the part of the troops, Soeur Marguerite tells a different story.*

Twenty men with a corporal and a sergeant lodged with thirty horses in the building of the Young Men's Congregation. They left these words written on the blackboard: 'The Germans fear God and no-one else in the world! Germany forever!' But where the opportunity presented itself, as in rue des Aveugles, it was quite otherwise. On Saturday 10 October, a road digger named Joseph Debrouwer was attacked by the Germans and killed with an automatic machine gun. The lawyer, Butaye, hidden behind a tree, had observed the sad spectacle.

As soon as the Germans were in the city, the bells of the different churches were silenced. They had demanded the freedom of the city for three days. The mayor, the aldermen and some prominent figures of the city were taken hostage. The city was forced to pay a sum of 70,000 francs; but there were only 65,000 francs in the coffers. Some German scouts and spies remained in the city.

On Tuesday, 13 October, an English army of 40,000 men entered the city: one section stayed there the night; another marched ahead of the enemy; a third was to follow it the next day.

On 14, 15 and 16 October, 250 British soldiers and 60 horses were housed in our convent. Since 9 October the cannon near Bailleul had not stopped roaring. On Saturday morning, around 11 o'clock, English soldiers had to leave the city in haste and the cannon thun-

---

* Explanatory and contextual historical text for the Diary is provided in sans serif type, as exampled here.

dered all day to the southwest. On Sunday, it was heard more in the south. Meanwhile, many French soldiers among which there were 40 clergy, attached to the ambulance service, had arrived at the riding school on rue de les Tuiles.[6] There were still many French and English soldiers in the city. Many refugees arrived from Roeselare and around Ypres. All the town's medical facilities, our school, the Sœurs de Marie, the local girls' school, the Meerseman house, were full to the eaves and presented the most harrowing scenes. This troop of men, women, old people and children, tired, weary, fleeing from one place to another in search of shelter, with anxious eyes, seemed to ask if here, at last, they could stop their sad flight. Oh! How they provoked our pity! But equally sadly they represented to us the desolation and the ruin of our poor country, yesterday so happy and so prosperous.

It was on 22 October that we were brought our first wounded, 300 British soldiers. Up to 5 November, we cared for up to 500. 9 English ambulances were here in succession until 5 November; from 12 to 15 December, it was the French who came, again replaced by English. Each ambulance stayed for 24 hours. I have to give testimony to the dedication of the British doctors and nurses who devoted themselves tirelessly, day and night, to healing their wounded, not taking any rest until the last one had received the necessary care. I have seen them staying at the operating table for 18 consecutive hours, content to eat something in their hands, from time to time. The kitchen of the cookery school served as an operating room. The first soldier to die with us was P. Whitehead, 2274, Batt. Regt. Chelmsford, Essex, England (died 22 Oct). Then Captain Lord Charles Fitsmaurice, 1st King's Dragoon Guards (died 30 Oct.) and Lieutenant A. D. Harding, Gloucestershire Regiment (died 30 Oct. 1914) before the 9th ambulance left.

On the evening of 27 October at about half past 10, several bombs were dropped on the city. The Carmelite Father, Père Jean, was wounded in his bed. In the home of Eugene Bonte, 3 children were wounded, including the eldest, Irma, quite seriously. There was extensive damage to Louise Devos' house in rue de Boudeurs. Several battles opened to the south and east, in Boesinghe, Zonnebeke, Hollebeke, Polygone and Hooghe.

On Wednesday 28th, at around two o'clock, we heard a great deal of tremendous cannon fire directed against two or three airplanes that were flying over the city dropping bombs, including one on the *Diamanterie* and another in Saint Joseph's school field.

On the morning of the 29th, more bombs were dropped: one fell on the Grand Place. In the rue Sainte-Elisabeth all the windows were broken. Valentine Dethoor who lived not far from the Sœurs de Marie, rue de Lille, had a leg and a foot crushed and died after receiving the last sacraments. Two children were killed, *rue de Thourout*.

For several days, I helped treat wounded Frenchmen (about 500–600) in the local girls' school, *rue de Lille*, with Sister Livine and Sister Elizabeth of the Soeurs Noires, and several young women of the town. Our Sister Philomena, Sister Marie Berchmans, Sister Germaine and two of the *Soeurs Noires* were also employed in the service of the wounded in the barracks where there were a lot of French and 80 Germans.

Among the wounded, there were only 3 Germans, including a nasty Prussian. He did not wish to drink or eat, believing that someone was going to poison him. He was only satisfied when he was served by the Sisters and he readily accepted what he was given. The other two were Bavarians, and decent boys. The French soldiers also loved the Sisters. Once we appeared in the room, it was: 'Dear Sister! Come and help me!' 'Make me comfortable!' 'But' I asked 'why didn't you ask the nurse who has just left?' 'Ah! Dear Sister,' they replied, 'they are rough and we prefer them not to touch us.' So, I said to myself, these are the men who, just a few years ago, drove out the poor French sisters from schools and hospitals! I have no doubt that they will be welcomed back after the war, now that the French have seen the priests and nuns at work.

During the following days, we were graced with a few bombs from time to time. It was worse on 3 November. Small *marmites* flew in large numbers in various parts of the city.[7] One struck the northern wall of the garden of the priest of St. Peter's, at about half past 10 in the morning. In the premises of the school of the *Soeurs de Marie* (our home) there was an English ambulance. The soldiers who were there thought that a shell had fallen on the convent. Glass shards were thrown onto the beds and everyone was seized with terror. I went to see what had happened. The convent was intact but a section of the priest's wall had collapsed, and in all the houses nearby, the windows were gone. At the home of the vicar, Reverend Leys, a large piece of iron had pierced the kitchen wall. A. Devos, a domestic assistant at the civil hospital, was killed outright. Near the Post Office, in the same street as the station, at the home of the French Sisters, and in many other places, these uninvited guests made their entrance.

As from 30 October, we considered it prudent to stay on the ground floor, now we spend nights in the cellar. Those who had no cellar took refuge in the casements.[8]

The ambulance had left us three days ago, leaving us eighteen dead. Fourteen could be buried in the civilian cemetery: others in the convent garden, the bombs would not allow us to carry them further. Towards evening we were brought a soldier who had been killed in the street. We buried him in the garden with his companions. A poor wooden cross bears the names of those who lie at rest, there.

Since 4 November, many of our Sisters have fled to Poperinghe. The sacristan, the choir, the organist, the organ blower, who hitherto had remained at their posts, made the same departure. Soon, there was only a dead and deserted city left, where shells continued to sow ruin and destruction. That same day, Oscar Seghers, who was at the door of his house, in the Place Van den Peereboom, had his head blown off; his two sons were seriously injured; and several British soldiers were killed in the street. At the Boudry home, rue Basse, a horse and a cow were hit the barn, etc.

Towards evening, things went a little quieter, until morning. Six more of our sisters left the city. In our convent there are only three or four Red Cross soldiers.

On 5 November, shells whistling almost incessantly for 9 hours and landing mostly on the west side of the city. The French wounded, with their ambulance service, left for Poperinghe. The city, with its shut-up houses, empties more and more, and seems so sad! The Taubes that have sent us their destructive bombs increase the terror and devastation still further. One bomb fell on the cemetery of St. Pierre, three or four metres from the church. The bombardment continued for much of the night and the whistling of shells in the darkness made things still more dismal. The next day, we could see further damage: the tower of St Martin's Church was destroyed. In almost every street, houses had collapsed and there were several deaths. In the 'Catholic circle' a few families were taking refuge in the cellars. Among them was the family Notebaert. Joseph, his wife, his six children and the maid were gathered in the cellar when, at about three in the morning, a shell burst there. Two children, the eldest, Albert and Gabrielle (20 and 22) were killed on the spot; Antoine, Anna and little Joseph were seriously injured. Mr Notebaert had a hand blown off. Mrs Notebaert, little Antoinette and the maid were saved. The leader of the 'Circle' also received serious injuries. Around five o'clock, Reverend Verriest arrived to request our assistance. Seeing the troubled-looking Reverend Mother – she dared not expose us to the danger, because the terrible bombing continued – I sensed her embarrassment and offered, myself, to take care of the misfortunate ones. 'Go ahead,' she replied, 'if you find a sister to accompany you.' I spoke to our good and virtuous Sr. Marie Berchmans who, after a moment's hesitation, accepted. We left in the grace of God, not without reciting, on the way, a good act of contrition. We ran like two mad women, from right to left, turning at every noise, and reached the cellar unharmed. Oh! the sad spectacle. Since three in the morning, the whole family had been there among the dead and the rubble. Other refugees who had sheltered with them in the cellar had fled. Firstly, the wounded had to be extracted, but we did not know where to begin. I went out into the street where I found four English soldiers. I took one by the arm and led him into the cellar: the others followed him. Not knowing the English language I could not speak to them, but it was not necessary, they saw soon enough what there was to do. They went to fetch two stretchers to take the wounded to our convent, where they received first aid from the good doctor Dieryckx.

6 NOVEMBER – From 8 a.m., the shelling started over again. It was dreadful! During the whole day, there was continual hissing and explosions. At about 1 o'clock, a shell fell on the path in front of the Dumont Blomme home, which is greatly damaged. Our convent also got its share: the big front door is collapsing and is full of small holes. All the windows of the facade are broken. Three people were injured, among them, Charles Beun to whom the priest of St. Pierre, who is everywhere where relief is needed, gave Extreme Unction. He died a few moments later.

Around 2 a.m., a large *marmite* made a deep hole in the cemetery of Saint-Pierre, opposite the entrance to the convent of the Soeurs Noires. All the windows in the neighbourhood were shattered. Dr. Dieryckx came to tend the wounded and to operate on them and the vicar, Reverend Leys, gave the last rites to Joseph Notebaert and his daughter Anna.

I am going to recount, here, a little incident that especially concerns our good sisters. The doctor needed a sister to assist him and I volunteered. 'Could I not have a more reliable person to help me?' he asked, a little warily. It was not long ago that I myself had passed through his hands for surgery. I ran to get Sister Marie Berchmans who was in the cellars with the other Sisters. The operation was about to begin, but the wounds were barely exposed when my fellow sister fainted. 'Lie down flat on the ground under the table,' the doctor told her, 'because we don't have time to take care of you.'

'Well, now,' I replied, 'the strongest of all! I think, doctor, that you will have to settle for the most reliable.'

So, we began (Mr. Notebaert's hand was severed) when, at about half past two, a shell fell on our convent and destroyed two classes,

10 metres from the cookery school where we were. Glass shards and stones came down on us and a large hole was made in the wall giving onto the rue Wenninck. The doctor had just made the last cut; we were both there, pale with fear, as in a cloud of smoke and white with dust. He was still holding the knife in his hand and me, the dismembered hand in mine. For a few seconds, we hesitated. The wounded were screaming and in a moment everything was upside down.

'Tut, tut, tut!' said Dr. Dieryckx, 'it's nothing! Let's continue our work, because we have no time to lose.' And with great calm, he set to work, giving a fine example of dedication and composure! Accident cases arrived from everywhere in the city. In front of the infantry barracks three people were literally blown to pieces. The bodies remained there until the following morning. In the 'Volkshuis' and the Chapel of St. Louis School, there was desolate ruin. That night the bombing slowed somewhat until Saturday morning; the night was fairly quiet.

On Saturday 7 November, at half past 4, there was a heavy bombardment. About one o'clock, a shell exploded in the garden of the Soeurs Noires, near the bakery. At the same time, Mr. Notebaert died in an alcove in the convent. A poor place! . . . but the safest at that moment. At the Church of St. Martin, the Dean alone remained. St. Nicolas' was closed. The priest is a military chaplain in our army; the vicars have left; we are left with the parish priest Delaere and the vicars R. Leys and A. Roose. In the afternoon the shelling resumed furiously. Eight more of our Sisters left Ypres, some for Boesinghe, others for Westvleteren or Poperinghe. All the separations were very painful. Not only the guns, but also the Taubes send their firebombs that cause new devastation on all sides: jets of flames rising towards the clouds and destroying everything, unconscious of the misfortunes and ruins that hatred makes them wreak. Houses burn in ten locations: rue du Temple, rue au Beurre, the Grand Place, rue de Dixmude, rue de Lille, everywhere, the same sad spectacle. The city looks like a huge furnace. The Church of St. Martin received a shell just like that of the Carmelite Fathers who, with the exception of Father Telesphore, fled the danger. A terrible night!

8 NOVEMBER – Shells and shrapnel. At the corner of rue de Crapaudières and rue de Boudeurs, a deep hole has been made. The Soeurs Noires and the Curé are doing their bit. Two houses to the west had collapsed. – Church services are continued on a regular basis, with the altar boy, Georges Cottenier, being very useful. Some of the Soeurs Noires left with the orphans. Three others with Miss Baus. The night passed relatively quietly.

9 NOVEMBER – Around 5 o'clock, the front-door bell woke us: the beautiful home of Mr. Fraeys Veubeke, rue au Beurre, was on fire. He had first been taken into the Creton home. The bombing is terrible. The shells being launched are very large. In Leet there is a new hole, deeply hewn, the tram tracks are broken without being bent or twisted and have been thrown some distance. The Ypertje is uncovered: a sizeable portion of the vaults has collapsed. (The Ypertje is a rivulet of the Iperlee flowing under several streets. Hence, the old adage: 'Ypres is built on a grid and will perish one Thuyndag'). We also received a 'souvenir'. In Sister Anna's cell, the lid of a shell blew the iron bed to pieces. This lid was about 32 centimetres in diametre and weighed 40 kg. It was about 4 o' clock. We were all gathered in the basement. The parish priest of St. Pierre had come to visit the injured and to console Mrs. Notabaert. At the same time, he said prayers for the deceased, Mr. Joseph Notebaert. Soeur Marie Berchmans accompanied him to the door, just as the 'souvenir' hit the convent. They were both hit on the head by several stones. Immediately, Sister Marie Berchmans returned to the cellar: 'Oh! Reverend Mother,' she said, 'the shell must have fallen here. I think it's a firebomb! I was just lying on a mattress, having a rest, because I had watched over the wounded all night.' She came towards me: 'I beg you, Sister Marguerite,' she said, 'come with me, I dare not go up alone.' As a precaution, we had put four buckets of water in the dormitories to extinguish fire, if needed. When we got to the second floor, we each took a bucket and we entered the cells, one by one. Dust blinded us, but we saw smoke coming out of Sister Ana's cell. We went in and saw a large opening in the ceiling and the bed broken into three pieces. The shell must have been there, but we could not find it . . . Suddenly, under the chair, I saw a sort of pan: I went to pick it up, but I almost burned my hand. 'Oh! It's the shell!' I exclaimed to myself. We doused it with our buckets of water and then, as the pan had slightly cooled, we picked it up to take it downstairs. But, on the way, it heated up again and we were afraid for a moment that it hadn't exploded! That is why we put it in a tub full of water! . . . We were afraid of the casing of a shell! . . . You see, we did not have much experience on the subject of these murdering things. The little women of the Belle hospice left today. In the old convent of the Pauvres Claires (New Museum), they have improvised a committee to deliberate on the measures to be taken in the city. The Rev. Dean Debrouwer is honorary president.

Mr. Stoffel is president.

Mr. Gravez Vice President.

Dr. Brutsaert secretary.

Camille Castel undersecretary.

A letter was written to inform the General Council in Poperinghe.[9] For two days we have been without bread or meat in the city. Many houses are burning, with the lack of firefighters. Theft and looting are taking place everywhere, and a group of volunteers has been organised as the Fire Service and Police.

The night was fairly quiet. However, shells continued to fall on the city. The Bank of Courtrai was consumed by fire. The school of Saint-Martin, together with the houses in the Old Clothes Market, and in the 'new' one in rue Saint-Jaques.

On the morning of 10 November, all was quiet until 8 o'clock, but after that the bombardment resumed with fury, especially in the St. Pierre district. The first houses in the rue des Chiens, near the rue Wenninck, were destroyed; a shell fell on the home of Mr. Bisschop. Around 10 o'clock, another shell knocked down part of the wall in the new sacristy and smashed a church window. As the parish priest, the vicar, Reverend Leys, and four other people were busy assessing the damage in the church, a new and formidable explosion occurred there; much of the arch above the altar of the Blessed Sacrament collapsed and shrapnel flew everywhere. – Maurice Lefebvre (20) was killed in front of the church, in the rue de Bouders; a woman, Emérence Wyckaert, was mortally wounded near the entrance of the church and carried into our convent. Those who were inside miraculously escaped. After the dust cloud dissipated we could see the huge hole left by the passage of the bomb: the altar was buried under the rubble. The confessionals, the tombstones, woodwork, chandeliers, walls, pavement, everything was destroyed. The electrics were out of order: the doors and the organ were smashed and shrapnel had blown through the door. Moments after the explosion, the parish priest noticed that the roof had caught fire near the hole made by the shell. Some men, armed with a fire pump connected to a nearby tank, and with water buckets supplied constantly by Sister Livine, Sister Genevieve and Sister Raphaelle, had to move quickly to quench the fire. The Tabernacle was under the rubble. In the afternoon, there was an attempt to uncover it. The parish priest and the vicar, Mr. Leys, tried to reach two ciborium containing the Blessed Sacrament. They were open and twisted and the Sacred Hosts scattered. With great care, the two priests were able to recover many of them. Were there any more? Of this they could not be sure. Eight days later, the parish priest found some more near the door of the sacristy. – An ugly disaster for the Church of St. Pierre recently restored and admired by everyone; irreparable loss and close to the pious heart of our venerated and good priest. However, he has not lost courage. 'God is watching over us,' he said.

In the afternoon, the bombing continued and caused great havoc in two houses in rue de les Riches-Claires. The church of Saint-Pierre being out of use, it is the small church of St. Godelieve which will serve as a parish church, although the roof and the ceiling each have a hole in them and the floor is covered in dust.

The Reverend Mother decided to leave the city today, with the remaining Sisters except Sister Marie Berchmans and Sister Marie. It was said that the Germans were going to enter the town and she did not want to leave young Sisters there. I had to follow in spite of myself.

We arrived, with our belongings, in Poperinghe, at the home of Sister Marie Joseph's parents where there were already six of our sisters. – In Ypres, the night was rough. The next day (11 November) at 5 o'clock in the morning, the vicar, Leys, was called to give Extreme Unction to a dying woman with the Sœurs Noires, whose convent is next to the vicar's house. The explosion of the night before, in the church of St Pierre, terrified the vicar. He had spent the night in the basement with the parish priest and had already packed his suitcase, resolved to leave the following day, no matter what. Around quarter past 5, a violent explosion was heard in the convent and in the priest's house. The parish priest, who was still in the cellar, was hit on the head by a piece of wood; he escaped safely through the battered doors.

The dormitory of the Sœurs Noires, where the old women and the infirm were, has collapsed. The parish priest of St. Peter had foreseen a misfortune and came in haste (he is always the first to arrive when help is needed). He was followed by a few men who I wish to mention here: Charles Backenlandt, Th. Kerrinckx and Jos. Cottenier.[10] Together they carried the old women to our convent. There were five deaths to lament: the good and holy vicar, Leys; the exemplary maid, Celine Pladys, and three little old women. The bodies were taken to the laundry room and then the injured were tended to. The Mother Superior was unconscious. She had been thrown some distance and was almost buried under the rubble. Only her feet were exposed and it was with great difficulty that she was extracted from under the debris. She had two ribs broken. Though injured herself, Sister Livine wished to help, but soon, weakened by loss of blood, which was considerable, she collapsed. An hour later, there was another explosion in the laundry room, the dead bodies that were there being thrown several metres away. The body of Celine Pladys was not found, although the search went on for three days. It was only found five months later, devoured by rats. – The parish priest, after this sad incident, found enough courage to say Mass in the bombed convent, after which he put in place some preventive measures against theft, in both the vicar's house and in the convent of the Sœurs Noires. He then had to bury the dead and evacuate the orphans. The injured Notebaert children were taken to Poperinghe with these, in a French auto-ambulance.

The bombardment continues violently. The parish priest spent the night in Charles Baus's cellar, as did Sister Genevieve and Sister Raphaelle of the Sœurs Noires. Sister Marie Berchmans and Sister Marie stayed with us, together with Miss Cloostermans. We also gave lodging to Mr. Frederick Harding, a Red Cross soldier, who helped treat the injured.[11] Miss Cloostermans and he had met Mr. G. W. Young, English commander of the Quaker ambulance which had lent them a motor car in which to transport the old women and orphans. It is through them that the parish priest was able to make contact with the 'Friends Unit'. From that day, Miss Cloostermans has been staying with us to help us.[12]

12 NOVEMBER – The parish priest and the two Sœurs Noires had just got up when an explosion was heard, followed by groans. The cellar door collapsed. It was light and so, to work! The Ameloot family, taking refuge in one of the cellars, was under the ruins. It was possible to save Maurice (16 years old), Madeleine (13), Yvonne (9) and Germaine (8). But the father, mother, grandmother and André (1) the baby, were nothing but horribly mutilated corpses. The next day we also found the body of Marie (11). As the bombardment went on, these children were taken to the hospital of St. Jean, with the injured from the day before, who were still at the convent. The two remaining Sœurs Noires also decided to flee the imminent danger. The parish priest came to ask for our hospitality. We are happy receive him! In the evening, at dinner time, the bell rang: a shell had just fallen on the cellar of A. Boone's brewery. There were two deaths: Charles Demey and Sophie Torens. The parish priest and Frederick Harding rushed to the disaster site, the first to give Extreme Unction, the second to heal the wounded. Mr. Torens was rushed to the hospital-hospice of Nazareth, the others to the Hospital of St. Jean. During the night, several explosions were heard in our neighbour-hood. The Braem family's home and the Ghesquière home in rue Lille, are destroyed.

13 NOVEMBER – The Holy Mass was said at the Hospice Saint Jean, as the parish priest is away finding a place for the homeless to

stay. He went, to this effect, to *l'Hospice des Aliénées* (the lunatic asylum) known as Sacré-Cœur, in the chaussée de Vlamertinghe, to see if they could receive the elderly and the injured, as the mentally ill had been evacuated to Vaucluse (France), under the custody of the Reverend Sisters and Dr. Dieryckx. Gustave Delahaye remained there as a janitor. The house had not been bombed. But, for some days, British soldiers had been staying there.

A few days ago we met Mr. G. W. Young, commander of the ambulance 'Friends Unit' that is doing a great deal of good for the people of Ypres, as well as for English and French soldiers. Thousands of people owe their lives to them, both among the people of Ypres and among those of the surrounding areas of Saint-Julien, Saint-Jean, Kemmel, Vlamertinghe, Poperinghe, Elverdinghe, Brielen, Woesten, etc.

This is what Commander G. W. Young wrote, on his arrival in our city:

Meanwhile, through all the varied beginnings and elaborations, Ypres remained our particular interest. Cars were frequently sent out along the bombarded road to see if a return there was yet possible, and on a memorable morning , only a week or so after our hurried night of occupation, I ventured once again in Cadbury's swift little grey car along the fatal road. The sky was clear, only an occasional shell screamed in the distance. The conflagrations were just over. The ruined towers stood gauntly against the sun. But as we entered and ran through the wrecked streets it seemed a city of the dead; scarcely a soul to be seen, and only a lost puppy or cat clamouring behind a door or grating. A chance meeting with a courageous girl, a daughter of one of the very few families that remained throughout the bombardment, revealed to us, however, a corner of the 'underworld' still persisting in the cellars. We learned of some seventy old alms people, unhappily left in the convent 'caves', and of the hundreds of children and miserable folk hidden in the darkness under the great earth fortifications. In a few hours we had fetched some dozen ambulances, loaded them up with the frail remnants of old folk, and watched the long procession wind safely out of the Gates, a strange sight in the deserted, battered streets, with the whistle and blast of the shells overhead as the only disturbance.[13]

While the parish priest and Miss Cloostermans (who takes very much to heart any task that she is allotted) were visiting the 'Sacré

Cœur', a shell fell on the hospital Saint-Jean, and another on the 'Nazareth', causing more fear than harm. In the afternoon, the 7th shell to fall on the civil hospital killed the maid, Leonie, Lèon Vanderbeke and two British soldiers. Others were wounded. At about half past 7 in the evening, at dinner time, a shell fell near the convent. Sister Marie Berchmans went to gather information: seven people were killed in the Saint-Louis school hall; Achilles Coutrez-Vanassche and three of her children: Remi (18), Gérard (9) and Antoinette (7); the only child of Mr. Degryse (8), Mr. Didier's nephew and an old man, Ch. Vereecke. Others escaped with injuries. Leonie Degrave had to have a leg amputated. At the Welfare Office, a shell; a few others on the Saint-Pierre cemetery broke several trees there. Seven passed over the convent during the night.

As from today, members of the Friends' Ambulance Unit will be active in our city, for as long as there remain citizens. Mr. G. W. Young wrote (later) on the subject:

> From this day on began our work in Ypres. Each day we returned with a doctor (Dr Rees at first) and sought out and looked after the wounded and sick in the scattered, dark, noisome cellars. In this work we were helped by a straggling R.A.M.C. soldier, 'Frederick', whose civilian ministrations could not save him in the end from a sharp punishment for shirking his real duties, but above all by the heroic Curé of St Pierre, Camille Delaere. This man's name deserves to be remembered as one of the real heroes of the war. He, practically alone, remained among his people, tending, consoling, joking, inspiring, helping, until the last penny was spent. His Church, only lately restored, was shelled four times: once he climbed onto the roof and himself cut out the burning rafters. His vicarage was wrecked. His curate was killed beside him. His own cassock was torn by flying fragments. The Convent St Marie, where he continued to lodge, with the angelic, ministering Soeur Marguerite and a few other Sisters, has five times been bombarded. But still his strong, aquiline, humorous face, his flying grey curls, his spare athletic figure in torn cassock move ceaselessly, night and day, among the people. His has been the powerful co-operation that has enabled us to carry out all our subsequent relief work for the town. There have been others, a few courageous and good men, but his has been the dominant personality. I have never worked with a man whom I could more heartily admire and like. But for him, we might never have overcome the suspicion and nervous terrors of the

reserved Flemish peasantry, or gained their confidence suffi-
ciently to get them to adopt our measures of precaution.[14]

14 NOVEMBER – Half past 7 and everything was still calm. This
horrible bombardment that has lasted for twelve days and has
caused ruins and victims, will it cease? Sister Ana and Sister
Elizabeth alone have remained at the civil hospital with forty-six
wounded Germans. They are almost without food and water,
because the Germans bombed the pipelines. And they cannot
abandon their wounded to get the necessary supplies; the bombing
is too violent. Dr. Dieryckx wrote to the commander of the place to
outline the situation and ambulance cars arrived in the evening to
evacuate the nuns and the injured. God only knows what these good
Sisters have suffered for twelve days and only He will reward them
as they deserve. The English battery has done a good job.

15 NOVEMBER – Mass at the Hospice of St. Jean at half past 6, by
Mr. Roose, High Mass at 8 o'clock, with the Blessed Sacrament, by
the Reverend Priest Delaere. He wished to say a few words to the
faithful, but emotion overcame him; he could not stop himself from
shedding tears. What a sad week! How many of his parishioners
have entered into eternity, and the good Mr. Leys was one of them!
    Although it has not yet suffered bombardment, the Saint-Jaques
church is closed. The priests of this church say Mass in large farms
or in barns out of town. In the afternoon, short-lived salvation. – At
night, we had to call the parish priest to administer the last rites to
an old man from Nazareth.

16 NOVEMBER – Everyone breathed more easily as if the previous
storms were to be followed by a lull. However, around 9 o'clock the
relentless bombardment resumed. I was in Poperinghe where there
was still no bombing. So, when I asked the Reverend Mother for
permission to return to Ypres, she consented on the condition that I
find a sister to accompany me. 'Two days without bombardment,'
she added, 'perhaps it means we're done for good and can we all
follow you in a few days.' Sister Antoinette and Miss Matilda Maroy
were very happy to leave with me, and we set off!
    How we reached the city unharmed, I do not know! For an hour
and a half, the bombing was intense! We met four to five hundred
refugees who begged us to retrace our steps, assuring us that we
were going to a certain death. We took no notice. With our skirts
rolled up, loaded with large packages and mud up to the knees, we
flew rather than walked, getting faster as we approached the city. We

brushed with death several times. We escaped with a few holes in our clothes made by shrapnel that exploded over our heads. Around 11 o'clock, we arrived at the convent where Sister Marie Berchmans and Sister Marie wept for joy upon seeing us. The good parish priest, hearing our voices, shouted: 'Ah! You've arrived just in time! There is work for you here!' Around half past 11, the rain of shells and shrapnel was less dense, yet still enough to maintain fear, because the shells had already caused a number of victims when they were least expected. Our little community here comprises the parish priest, Delaere, Sister Marie Berchmans, Sister Marie, Sister Antoinette and me, and Mathilde Maroy.

17 NOVEMBER – While we were being bombarded, a small woman came to tell us that Dean Debrouwer was sick. Sister Marie Berchmans and I went to give him the necessary care and to leave him everything he needed for the night, because the Dean lacked everything, since he did not want to stay in his home. He was down in the New Museum, lying on a mattress and suffering a good deal.

18 NOVEMBER – Successive shells and shrapnel bombs. During the Committee meeting, a shell fell on the New Museum and knocked down one of the turrets. Fortunately, the cassock and the hat of the parish priest were the only casualties. In the morning, the Dean of Poperinghe arrived in an ambulance to collect the Dean of Ypres. All the priests of St. Martin also left. I told them that Saint-Nicolas had long been closed. – This evening shrapnel killed a horse in Goemaere's stable.

19 NOVEMBER – Towards noon, increased intensity, especially towards the station and Malou Boulevard. Will there be nothing left of our beloved city?

20 NOVEMBER – shrapnel, shells and firebombs at 8 o'clock, mostly over *les Halles*. The house of the chemist, Carpentier, is in flames. Some firefighters, in the Place Vanden Peereboom, were trying to extinguish the fire when a shrapnel bomb exploded, killing Arthur Deweerdt and injuring Emile Cylor and Eugene Slosse. Jules Garreyn, who went to the Belle Hospice in search of bread, was also killed outright. – (Bakers left their bread at the Hospice Belle, where residents could buy it, which had a double advantage: the bakers were paid and the bread was distributed economically). The parish priest gave conditional Extreme Unction to the victims. The injured were brought to us where Miss Cloostermans and I gave them first

aid until the arrival of the doctor of the Friends' Ambulance Unit.[15] From 3 o'clock, a little bit of calm, that was soon replaced by the din of the bombing and the English cannon raging. I can therefore, at my ease, also make noise, because I have to repair the priest's shoes, which have been sorely tested by pieces of brick and glass! Three boots of English officers, who had died with us, provided me with a pair of suitable shoes. The work is not the finest, nor the nails, but they will be strong!

21 NOVEMBER – Many houses are destroyed, rue de Lille, rue de Trèfles, the Old Clothes Market.

22 NOVEMBER – The last Sunday of the liturgical year. The Gospel speaks of the devastation of Jerusalem and the end of the world! A sad image of that which prevails in our poor city! What will remain of the ancient splendour? Towards 6 o'clock the next morning, the bombing was in full flow! Around 9 o'clock, *les Halles* was bombarded. The first shell fell on the tower, the third on the clock. Around 11 o'clock, the bell tumbled and *les Halles* was on fire. It was a horrible sight! Soon the building would be nothing but a large blaze. The tower of St. Martin's church caught fire. The priest got there around 6 o' clock and entered the sacristy in the sanctuary; the roof of the nave and the Chapel of the Holy Sacrament was in flames. With the help of Mr. Frederick Harding, Miss Cloostermans and a Belgian brigadier, he managed to save several former antependiums including one from the twelfth century. They have been taken to the Boerenhol inn. I arrived just in time to help save some beautiful rugs and statues, which were carried into the third sacristy. The most valuable objects were removed from the Halles and taken either to the 'Boerenhol', or to the Hotel Chatellenie or to the cellar in the home of the mayor, Mr. Colaert. The parish priest went begging for a little water. With some difficulty, he obtained two buckets which he took to the church. With a wet cloth, he managed to smother the fire that had reached the pulpit. Some French soldiers, at rest that day, also helped in the rescue, especially in *les Halles*. At around 8 o'clock, at the table in the kitchen, we were sharing the disasters of the day, to the light of the flames that continued their work of destruction, when Sr. Marie Berchmans asked if anyone had saved the statue of Our Lady of Thuyne. We could not remember having seen it; it was to be assumed that she remained on her usual throne in the church. We would have to return, as tomorrow it would probably be too late. The parish priest, however, thought that we had done enough work for one day and wanted us to wait until the next

day; but we insisted, saying that it was our duty to save the good Virgin of Thuyne who, for almost a hundred and fifty years, had been carried in procession by our Sisters, she was the patron of the city, etc. We insisted so much that the priest agreed to let us go. The bombing was terrible. We passed under the 'Niewwerck' which was on fire. On the way, we met the brave sergeant who had helped us and he accompanied us. In his childhood he had been an altar boy at St. Martin. The force of the exploding bombs was such that we had to lean against the church wall for half an hour. Around 9 o'clock we could enter. The sparks were falling on us and chunks of burning wood landed at our feet. To our regret, we could not find the statue of Our Lady of Thuyne. So, we took the 'Thuyne' (its pedestal). Someone must have put the Virgin somewhere safe. After cutting a painting from its frame and taking some items to the third sacristy we went first to Chatellenie, then to Boerenhol and to the mayor's basement, but nowhere did we discover the statue, and we returned very sad to the convent, where we found the parish priest, Sister Marie and Sister Antoinette in prayer. We had a vague feeling that something sad would happen to us. This morning, the Belle Hospice received a shell when I was passing by – a minute later and I would have been under the rubble. Towards evening the beautiful museum was, in turn, kindled. Ah, no! There will be nothing left of all the treasures, collected with such great effort. What a sight, sad and grandiose at the same time! But everything is going! *Les Halles*, churches, homes are consumed and the bodies are piling up. Stop, murderers! Stop your work of destruction! Tell me! Why do you make your sacrilegious hands weigh down on our beloved sanctuaries? The richesse and munificence of our old town does not stop you? Well! At least, spare our poor people who have done you no harm!

23 NOVEMBER – In the morning, despite the danger, the parish priest returned to make sure there was nothing he could save. Of *les Halles* and the Town Hall, only the walls are left. The Cathedral continues to burn; much of the nave has already collapsed. The new museum, Parnassus and the butchers' market form a huge blaze and there is no thought of extinguishing the fire, as there is a lack of both manpower and water. The abbot Versteele managed to open the safe in the sacristy at St. Martin's. The parish priest carried the Blessed Sacrament to the convent school of St. Joseph, where, with the help of some French soldiers, everything was put in a safer place, in the cellar. Scaffolding near the sacristy caught fire, but we were able to put it out. So we hope that the sacristy, where there are many valu-

ables, will remain untouched. – We learned that Mr. Vander Ghote, the engineer, has saved the statue of Our Lady of Thuyne and is keeping it his house, on the Menin Road. It is not safe there, and we are going to reclaim it. Vander Ghote is giving it to us voluntarily and is even going to bring it himself to the convent. – The other half of the rue au Beurre is on fire! It's horrible! So, when will it end? Because the bombing always continues. From 5 o'clock to half past 6, 11 shells fell in the city. – Following the Committee meeting, the parish priest went to Boerenhol where he found four French cars, loaded with all that could be saved from *les Halles* and Saint Martin's Church. 'Hello!' exclaimed the priest, 'where are you taking it, and with what permission?' 'To Berck-Plage,' was the reply, 'with permission of the mayor.' The parish priest protested in vain. They promised a receipt, which was not given, and left. – Some time later we read in a French newspaper that two French officers had rescued the treasures of Ypres, including the Virgin of Thuyne. This news had even resulted in a poem composed by a Franciscan nun. How absurd! These gentlemen had not faced the flames. And the figure that was believed to be that of the Virgin was simply a statue of St. Barbara! The real statue had been in our cellar for three weeks, then, upon the order of the parish priest, she was placed in our chapel until it was bombed. It was then taken back down the cellar, with our other statues, and remained there until 9 May 1915, when she was brought to us by the parish priest of Poperinghe. The following June, the parish priest brought it to me (together with other items found) at the boarding house Saint-Denis, Place Saint-Jean, in Saint-Omer, instructing me to put everything in a safe place. – On the afternoon of the 23rd, around 2 o'clock, I went to the corner of rue Wenninck, to cast a glance over our steaming *Halles*, when, in the distance, I saw two men arrive. The first wore the garb of a cattle dealer and swam around in his loose clothes; the second wore clothes that were too short, like a schoolboy. They advanced, looking this way and that, as though to assess the damage caused. I was very surprised to meet strangers at that time because for three or four days there had been almost no people in the city. I waited until they noticed me. They surveyed me from head to foot and then I heard steps behind me, it was Maertens who had been to find some food. They asked him: 'Friend, can you tell us which side the shells are coming from?' – 'I know nothing', Maertens said, while running, 'if you want to know, listen! It's not good in this street!' I met Charles Backenlandt and his son and I asked if they had noticed the two individuals. 'Yes,' answered Paul, 'and I think they are both odd.' 'Come on, Charles,' I said, 'make a signal to stop that French truck over there!' It stopped and we told the two soldiers who were in it of our suspicions. One of the two placed his revolver beside him, then they went hastily on their way. They soon reached the two men and went to warn the guard at the Lille Gate. The two walking suspects were arrested as German spies.

24 NOVEMBER – At one o'clock in the morning, the doorbell woke us up. A shell had fallen in the dormitory of the old women in the Saint-Jean hospice. The parish priest, Sister M. Berchmans, Miss Cloostermans, Frederick and two soldiers encountered *en route*, went there. I stayed at the convent to receive the wounded. What chaos! They could not distinguish the beds, all buried under the rubble. With great care, the little old women were taken away. Marie Gaston had died; another had a crushed foot. Six others, injured, were anointed with holy oil and received absolution from the priest. While clearing up, the corpse of another old woman was found, a refugee from Zillebeke. In the absence of men and a vehicle, the dead were buried in the garden with two other bodies, brought last Saturday from Zillebeke, by two French soldiers.

The bombardment does not stop. The ground shakes while one seeks a little rest during the night. What a state our unhappy city is in! It is heartbreaking. Sister Marie Berchmans went to Poperinghe to ask that all the old people from the hospital be taken there. To stop the thefts, the Committee will ask for police and soldiers. During the night three houses on rue de la Bouche collapsed. No new casualties, fortunately!

25 NOVEMBER – Around half past 5 this morning a shell fell on the Post Office and did great damage, but there were no major injuries. Around 6 o'clock the Reverend Mr. Roose, expected to say mass, did not arrive. We knew that he was taking refuge in the basement of the Post Office with his elderly mother. Georges Cottenier went there to find out the cause of the delay. No one could leave the cellar without outside help; therefore, the first concern was to free those who were there. Mr. Roose was no longer safe in this place, and came and asked us for hospitality for him and his mother. This poor woman had not left the cellar for a fortnight. With us, however, it is quite the contrary, we are only here to sleep or during a major bombardment in our area. – About 10 o'clock, in front of Mr. Roose's house, rue de Lille, a shell fell and shattered all the front of the house, smashing the contents. We were very concerned about Mr. Roose, who had had to go there to find a knitting book for his mother, and poultry feed.

By chance, or rather by the effect of divine Providence, he had met the parish priest who had instructed him to go immediately to the Cœur des Veuves [widows' home] order to help an old woman. – While I tended a wounded man, large stones were blown from all sides. One fell on the Nazareth, one in the Chapel of the Sœurs Noires, on the Communion bench, and three in our convent. A relative calm succeeded this dreadful noise and lasted all day. Many people died in Saint-Jean hospice, as a result of their injuries. In the afternoon, the car of the Friends' Ambulance Unit, sent by Commander Young, transported six women to the hospital Sacré Coeur and eight to the Sœurs Paulines in Poperinghe.

26 NOVEMBER – Two homes burned during the night. No shells, but occasionally shrapnel comes to increase still further the number of injured. In the afternoon, violent shooting: a great fight took place near the city. Around 3 o'clock the Quakers' motor cars returned to get the old women still remaining in the Saint Jean, and the elders of Nazareth. They will be driven to Poperinghe and from there to France.

27 NOVEMBER – Several shrapnel bombs; two British soldiers were killed and four injured near Mr. Verschoore's laundry. The devices fell mainly near the station.

28 NOVEMBER – Great noise of guns and cannons. Six shrapnel bombs burst over the city. The last of the old men of Nazareth and some old invalids were taken by the Quakers.

The corpses deposited in the garden of the Saint-Jean hospice were dug up and brought to the civil cemetery. Towards evening, the sound of guns and cannons dissipated. Josephine Cloostermans is suspected as a spy!! She who does so much good here!! What bizarre incidents are caused by the war.[16]

I forgot to tell about an incident that happened just days after the Cathedral fire. We were without bread in the convent and it was already rare to find bread or flour in the city. So I went to my father's house, in the commercial quarter, to see if I could procure any. He could give me two loaves, promising to give me more the next day. In going, I passed the tomb of Commander de la Croix, of the 114th division. On my return I met Auguste Louf, who informed me that the reliquary attached to the wall in the church of St. Martin had been smashed by a shell and that the French soldiers were removing 'souvenirs'. I informed the parish priest who told me to warn Mr. Lorrain, of rue Thourout. I went, but found no one at home, and the parish priest ordered me to go myself to the church when I had time. Around 4 o'clock I went in a blue apron and clogs and armed with a hammer and tongs. Sister Antoinette took a bag to put the relics in. There were three or four French soldiers in the church. One of them took the doors of the reliquary off for me. Some relics and the seal had already disappeared. I climbed the high altar; but I could not reach the top. We took away the precious relics. The soldier followed us carrying the two doors, which are not without some artistic value. Upon leaving the church, a wall collapsed, either by the force of the wind or by a falling shell, as the bombardment continued. The next day we found the vault of the great nave destroyed. Fortunately, the collapse did not happen during our operations yesterday. It is amazing how you get used to everything, even to the bombing. During one of those terrible hours when the guns were doing their work of destruction, we saw a good old woman come out of her house armed with a broom, quietly sweep away the debris that the collapse of the house next door had just scattered on the road, blocking the way, and then return to her house to sit out the crisis, without appearing to suspect that she herself might at any moment increase the number of victims.

29 NOVEMBER – Around midnight, a frantic ringing of the door-bell woke us up. Sister Marie Berchmans opened the door and returned in haste to the basement. Urgent help was requested. Miss Cloostermans and I got up immediately. What had happened? Velghe Carlier had fought two British soldiers and a few civilians and had received multiple stab wounds. 'Once is enough! Do you hear, Velghe?' I said, 'we need our dressings for those injured by the bombs and not for those who fight.' From 8 in the morning to 2 in the afternoon, shrapnel were being launched on the city. Around 11 o'clock, the parish priest told me to go to rue Cannon and No. 3 rue Nazareth to collect two old women, as at 3 o'clock the Friends would come with their ambulances to take away the elderly and invalids. As that neighbourhood had just been bombed, I asked him to let me wait for a lull. 'Go right now,' he replied, 'these poor people might be forgotten later on, and their life may depend on it.'

'In the name of God,' I said to myself, and I left. But no sooner had I taken a few steps in the street when . . . sss . . . sss . . . bang! The head of an explosive bomb rolled into the street, close to me. I ran back. Sister Marie, who was still at the entrance, said, 'How glad I am not to have to go!' But the parish priest heard the sound of my voice and, from the kitchen, shouted: 'Well! Have you still not left?' Three times I tried to go but had to turn back almost as quickly. Finally, I grew bolder and returned this time with the little old women, who I took to the convent. No less than five shrapnel bombs passed over our heads, and you can believe my heart was beating . . . But it was from that day that I became more courageous in facing the bombing. Here, as elsewhere, it is only the first step that is difficult. Around 2 o'clock the Friends' cars arrived. The parish priest made a point of accompanying all the little old ladies and little old men who were with us, and took them to the Pénitentines of Poperinghe, until he could accommodate them adequately in France.

30 NOVEMBER – The night was fairly quiet. Between 7 o'clock in the morning and 2 o'clock in the afternoon, several exploding bombs reached us. However, in the morning, the French guns and rifles made a great racket in an attempt to gain some ground. Time for *marmites*. A man was killed in boulevard Malou, by shrapnel from an exploding bomb.

1 DECEMBER – It looks like the fight is a little less furious. Only the whistling of some shrapnel bombs disturb the rest of the night. Emile Lagrand is the first operated on by Dr. Rees and the medical assistants Harvey and Tarpe of the Friends' Ambulance Unit. The operation was carried out in the sewing room of the convent of the Sisters of Lamotte. Today, the parish priest left with the Quakers' ambulance to seek shelter for wounded civilians. They returned via Woesten, where the Friends installed an ambulance service several days ago. Too bad they are not closer to Ypres, where there would be more work to be done. But the parish priest found a good way of bringing them to us, because the Quakers ask nothing more than to be able to do as much good as possible. Today some shells fell in the vicinity of the hospital of St. Jean. A man was hit near the station.

2 DECEMBER – Night and day were calm. The parish priest went to Poperinghe, this time in search of the Sisters of the civil hospital because G. Young, of the Friends, agreed to open a hospital for wounded civilians, provided that the parish priest finds a location not far from the city and some Sisters to help. 'We must strike while the iron is hot,' said the parish priest 'and the earlier the better. Because it is so far to go to get help from the Quakers in Woesten or Poperinghe.' So, in the evening, the parish priest returned with Sisters Aloysia and Antonia, from the civil hospital. They went to the Sacré Coeur because our good pastor, before leaving this morning, spoke with the concierge Gustave Deahaye, and the Friends had

already been there for some hours. Here is the report of the commandant G. W. Young, on the ambulance service established in the Sacré
Coeur, rue Vlatmeringhe:

After a few days it became evident that we could do little to save
the wounded in the darkness and damp of the cellars. We had to take
the grave responsibility of collecting them into some central room
above ground. Here again fortune favoured us. The Curé piloted us
to one of the great asylums on the edge of the town that had escaped
damage. The steward smiled at our request. 'I knew they must come
to me for a hospital sometime,' was all he said. Through the barrack
quarters of some 3,000 soldiers, he led us by a series of locked doors
in a maze of buildings and threw open the door of a ward,
untouched, clean, unsuspected, unpillaged, all but ready for use!
This was our famous 'Gustav', our second great stand-by, a man who
has done all he has promised up to time (in war!) and whose stories
and inventive genius seem inexhaustible. His five pretty children
and good wife have been with us through all the dangers since that
time. Not for one day has he left his charge of the great Institute
placed in his care. His varied services and successful dealings, with
intrusive authorities of four nationalities, would fill a book. At 11
o'clock we entered. By 12 we had fitted up the stoves etc. By 1 o'clock
the Curé had fetched us two nursing sisters from Poperinghe. By 2
the beds were ready. At 2.30 we moved in the first cases. Surely few
hospitals have ever been opened at shorter notice! – These sisters
deserve further mention. Sister Aloysia and Sister Antonia came
first. Then as the work grew, Sisters Anna, Madeleine, Julienne,
Elisabeth. Lastly, Sisters Godelieve and Marie and the Old R. Mother,
splendid, vigorous, humorous, sympathetic Flemish women, caring
for nothing but work and full of fun. They are the Sisters of the civil
Hospital.[17]

3 DECEMBER – The night was quiet. Could the storm have passed?
No, alas! Around 9 o'clock, a real rain of shells began. Fortunately,
the dressings were done, as Dr. Rees was very early this morning. As
of 25 November, there had not been any shells on the city, but this
afternoon quite a few *marmites* arrived. Around 2 am, a shell fell on
Doctor Dieryckx's kitchen, killing Mrs. Lazeuse, two of her children
and an old woman. How fortunate, again, that the Quakers could
come so soon to help us! They carried three injured to hospital while
we took care of the dead. At the Kruisstraat three soldiers were killed
near the bridge. The cannonade seems to have come mainly from the
north side of the city.

So far, the Committee has held one session per day. As from today, there will be three meetings a week. Curé Delaere, Mr. Lapierre and Dr. Van Robaeys have also joined the Committee.

4 DECEMBER – The bombing continues. Several medium sized shells fell near the station and the Verschoore laundry. The house of Mr. Morlion, Malou Boulevard, is on fire. At the Kruisstraat, French troops were preparing to leave for the trenches when a German airplane on reconnaissance gave a signal (small sparks escaping from the machine) and immediately the shells came: ten soldiers were killed and many wounded. Treachery is suspected and it is said that a German spy was hidden in the laundry with a wireless device.

Now that the wounded civilians have their hospital, the parish priest is responsible for finding a home for the aged. The doctors and assistants of the Friends Unit work with admirable dedication. Opened just two days, their hospital already has two wards for wounded: one for women and one for men. Tonight, the guns thundered again. The noise is such that it might be compared to that that would be made by the enormous and unending unloading of large stones.

5 DECEMBER – A fairly quiet night. The sound of guns has decreased and seems to be more distant. The wounded that are not in the hospital can come to the convent for treatment from Miss Cloostermans or from me, under the supervision of Dr. Rees and Dr. Malabar, of the Friends. In the evenings, we visit those too scared to come to the convent. Thus, almost every night we have to do our tour of the cellars and casements – What are the casements in Ypres? They are underground spaces beneath the ramparts, where residents who do not have well-conditioned cellars can take refuge. Every family chooses its little corner and installs two or three mattresses, two or three chairs, a small lamp, sometimes a small table and a kerosene stove. The heavy entrance door is partially closed. It is not surprising, then, that after some time, contagious diseases break out. People have remained for six weeks in this reduced space, without seeing daylight. One day, I found a two-month child that was born there, and had not yet breathed clean air from outside.

The Quakers' ambulance collected four elders and a tubercular case to take them to the Sacré Coeur in rue Thourout.

6 DECEMBER – Around midnight, more than 50 shells fell in the city, then everything went quiet. In the afternoon, three or four shrapnel bombs and a small *marmite* exploded in our neighbour-

hood. At night, the sound of gunfire again became very loud, always coming from the same place.

7 DECEMBER – The first part of the night was quiet, then at 11.30 it rained shells that exploded very noisily, shaking the ground. In our cellar, we felt as though we were on the tray of a scale. Around 12.00, I heard footsteps in the corridor. I went to check with Sister Marie. It was a man coming to ask for our assistance; a shell had fallen on the inn 'Het Zeepaard' in rue de Boudeurs. The whole family was under the rubble; one of Joseph Hoff Coffyn's children is dead, several others injured. The parish priest, Frederick (the English soldier) and Melle Cloostermans went there immediately. I got together some necessary items for dressings. 'Monseigneur le curé has just arrived,' said a man. A second shell must have fallen on the church, because sparks were coming out of the roof. The parish priest ran into the street and saw that, indeed, the church had begun to burn. The most urgent attention was given to the wounded and we left them in the care of Frederick and Miss Cloostermans, who took them to the casements for the night. The parish priest and I ran to the convent in search of the keys to the church. But, because of the state of panic we were in, we could not find them. The priest sent me to look in the basement, while he himself went for Mr. Angillis and Jos. Cottenier who managed to break down the door of the tower with a large hammer. Meanwhile, the church door was also opened in the same way. A shell had fallen through the roof, behind the pulpit, and had done great damage. Mr. Angillis felt that it was necessary to put out the fire by climbing onto the roof, but no one dared to venture there. The priest went up himself. Jos. Cottonier and two volunteer firemen followed his example. I tried to follow them, with two buckets of water, when my double burden was suddenly taken from me, though I could not see who had taken my load. I imagine their contents must have diminished somewhat, because from the convent to the church there are at least 300 metres and the road had been made slippery and uneven by snow and ice. With this, the deafening noise of shells falling in the area, then a dark and unfamiliar staircase! . . . Sister M. Berchmans, Sister Marie and Sister Antoinette also followed, each carrying two buckets of water. One of the Sisters rang the church bell; three other firefighters: Declercq, D'Hollandere and another who had witnessed the bombardment arrived with buckets, shouting: 'Water, *s'il vous plait*! Water!' Eight women came out of the casements in response. The men were afraid! Mr. Roose, the vicar, put them to work in carrying 800 chairs, found under the blazing roof in the nave of Saint Pierre, to the nave of Notre Dame.

A French commander had heard the sound of the bell from the trenches. He sent an officer to enquire as to what had happened. In short, I told him of the accident and he entered the church for a moment, to see what was happening. 'Courageous women!' he said, then went back.

The shells continued to arrive while we were looking for water. Thankfully, around 2 o'clock, without further incident, the fire was extinguished and everyone went back to their dark shelters . . . Ah! What a mess our church is in! I had just reached the convent when I heard footsteps in the corridor. Three men from the Grimonprez household, opposite the church, were injured, and came to seek attention. Having no cellar, they were sleeping in the back kitchen, when a shell fell on the house. As they were speaking to us, a shell whistled overhead and struck the chimney which rolled onto the glass roof. We rushed into the kitchen! There, I began dressing the two who had head wounds and a third who had been hit in the leg. None of them dared to go home. Josephine Cloostermans led them into the basement of Mr. Gillebert's brewery, opposite the convent. Another shell had wounded Mr. Degryse. He had a wound 5 cm. long. I dressed it until it could be sewn by Dr. Manning, of the Quakers. Two shells also fell on the home of the parish priest; thankfully, he was with us. Yet another fell on the convent of the Soeurs Noires, where everything was broken all over again. The house of Mr. Herman, our Director, received one, as well as that of Slembrouck, the baker, and Mr. Verhaeghe, of Biekorf. All this was in our neighbourhood. This night was, for us, also the most terrible. There were 15 new casualties. – In the morning they came to tell us that four people from the street Dixmude had been killed and three others wounded. Miss Cloostermans went to tend to the latter. Later in the day, we heard talk of many other victims. During the night, three or four shells passed over us. In the evening, the cannons and guns had been making a great row and we supposed that a violent battle was about to take place. It was said that the rain and the cold weather had forced the Germans to abandon their trenches and they had lost a lot of ground and men.

8 DECEMBER – Can we not get some respite from the good Blessed Virgin or her divine Son on this great day of celebration?[18] The night was calm and the peaceful rest has done us much good. – In the morning nothing happened until 9 o'clock, but from then until noon, twelve shells landed in the city. In the afternoon three more shrapnel bombs. At night, the sound of gunfire was somewhat lighter. Today, I went to give information to many mothers who wished to be taken

to Furnes with their families. By 11 o'clock, the dining hall and corridor were full of women and children waiting for the ambulance cars of the Friends' Ambulance Unit. Before leaving, Sister M. Berchmans gave them all a plate of rice with milk and toast.

9 DECEMBER – After a night and a morning of calm, some shrapnel bombs were launched from half past 3 to half past 4. The injured took advantage of the calm to come to renew their dressings. Before the arrival of the doctor, 25 dressings had already been changed. A good man, a refugee from Zonnebecke, Ed. Deleu, came to ask me to look at his chin. It was awful to see. After he was examined by Dr. Manning, I promised to take care of him myself if he could come twice a day, which he promised to do. So, I began by cutting off his beard.

10 DECEMBER – It was not until half past 3 in the afternoon that a dozen shrapnel bombs arrived. In the evening, escorted by a Dominican Father of Jerusalem who had said Mass in the morning in the chapel of the Soeurs Noires, a sub-lieutenant, and a novice of the Society of Jesus, a cart brought us the corpse of a French captain. The Germans had taken a trench near Zillebeke, and we had removed them almost immediately. During this recovery, captain Diedelge, of the 126th, was hit. Today, a great number of citizens of Ypres, including many sick and injured, were taken to Furnes.

11 DECEMBER – After a quiet night, shrapnel rained down in the morning, from 6 o'clock to 7 o'clock and from 2 o'clock in the afternoon. More than 40 exploded in the city. In the evening, cannons and guns made a terrible racket! A new fight must be engaged.

12 DECEMBER – During the night, no explosion was heard. It was only in the evening from 5 o'clock to half past 5 that several large shrapnel bombs and some *marmites* exploded. One fell on the Nazareth convent where sick French soldiers were at rest. Eight were killed and many others wounded. The couple Eu. Vanuxem-Duflou and two of their children also received injuries, a shrapnel bomb having fallen on their house. A third knocked down the remains of the Georges Roscamp-Coffyn home. Father, mother and three children were buried under the rubble. Many people in rue Basse were injured. A bomb exploded near the casements and a wooden house; husband, wife, elderly mother and two children of the Cam Velghe-Carlier family were injured; a third child was killed outright. We were brought the Vanuxem-Duflou and Devos wounded to dress.

Meanwhile, Miss Cloostermans went to the casements to treat the Velghe family, while the parish priest went to the Roscamp-Coffyn residence. All his efforts to save the victims were in vain. After two hours of searching through the rubble, five bodies were pulled out. What pain for the good parish priest who so loves his parishioners! We asked the Quakers to come to the convent and to the casements to get the most seriously injured. – The Germans, we are told, had to abandon three trenches. Could this terrible bombardment be a result of their impotent rage? – In the evening, a French medical unit came, just before the evening bombing. The doctor was not very civil towards us. He wanted to have at his disposal the middle classroom, where we had stored all the furniture from the convent that had been saved from the bombing. It was quarter to 6, and by 6 o'clock everything had to be ready to receive the troops. It was politely pointed out that this was totally impossible and he would have to settle for the large recreation room where there was a good stove and where the broken windows had been patched. So, Sister Antoinette and I prepared the room. When the soldiers came at around 6 o'clock, they were delighted to find a good heated room, they could not thank us enough. – Around half past 6, French cannons thundered loudly. The Germans did not fail to respond.

13 DECEMBER – The night was quiet, but in the morning the guns were thunderous! In the afternoon, several of these dreadful shrapnel bombs fell, exploding up to three, four times. In the evening, the sound of cannons started over again while machine guns and rifles joined in. The noise became deafening.

14 DECEMBER – Quiet until about 7 a.m., and then the French cannons roared with fury: a dreadful fight began! It must be terrible on the battlefield. It's impossible to make yourself heard in our kitchen. Around 8 am, the German guns replied. Several shells fell in our neighbourhood. Our convent received four in 7 minutes. Fortunately, the French soldiers were not in the classroom that the doctor had so urgently required, as many would have paid with their lives: this room was found completely destroyed. No one was hit in the hall, only a door was knocked down. The first shell had found me at the sewing machine, employed in joining some strips of bandage. All the windows of the work room were shattered; a shower of stones and glass fell on my back; all our pharmacy store, which was on the table, was smashed. In an instant, without knowing how, I found myself in the corridor, where I was welcomed by a big board, the seat of a school-desk, which came down on the back of my head. Another

jump and I was in the kitchen where I found Sister M. Berchmans, transfixed, pale with fright . . . sss! bang! A second shell fell in front of the classroom door, next to the kitchen. Sister Marie and Miss Cloostermans threw themselves quickly into the kitchen, all covered with dust from fallen bricks. We could not see anything there for a while and we stayed in the cellar, all four of us, to sit out the storm. The already-bombed classroom received the third bomb and the fourth exploded in the shed and the chicken coop. Others fell on the Van Campo home, on the corner of rue Crapaudière, on Mr. Werbrouck's store at the entrance of our nursery school, rue Sainte-Catherine, near the Saint-Jacques church, rue Dixmude etc. – When the first shell fell on the monastery, the soldiers were scared. Some fled and one of them was killed near the door. The parish priest had time to administer Extreme Unction, the poor man had his legs blown off. Yet another was struck near the Lille Gate, in front of the Lalou house, and Mr. Devarvere, rue Dixmude. The wounded were, among others: two of the Borremans sisters, of the *Cour des Veuves*; Declercq, a volunteer firefighter, and Louis Vandevelde, etc. The aid station of the 94th was forced to leave our convent and take refuge in the cellars of the Gillebert brewery. What amazes us is the childish fear of some of the Red Cross soldiers. They flee at the slightest noise, hiding, shaking and jumping into the pits at the cackle of a hen! Others, however, are full of courage and composure. In the afternoon: visit of some shrapnel and small shells. Today, we have to patch up doors and windows, nailing in some places for, besides the shells, there are still gentlemen thieves who make home visits! And this is how, this time, I became a carpenter. And you need nails. I have already used no less than 1½ kg large and 2 ½ kg small.

In the evening, a new clash of arms.

15 DECEMBER – Shells arrived in the city three times during the night. Around half past 9, three or four shells; 4 o'clock, six or seven shells; around 5 o'clock, three shells. They fell everywhere and have caused quite a lot of damage. However, no human lives to mourn; not even injured!

Early morning, we had to start cleaning our new small pharmacy and board up the windows of the sewing room. During the day, several shells exploded here and there. It seems that the Germans suffered some losses. How I wish it were true and that we were soon freed from these murderous gunfights!

16 DECEMBER – Everything is peaceful and one can barely hear a few shots in the distance. In the morning, some shrapnel on the

Welfare School and on the station. Then all of a sudden, at about 3 in the afternoon, a succession of half a dozen of these horrible explosive shrapnel bombs. The shells that the Germans sent us today did not explode (they must be the ones they bought from the French in Maubeuge.) When the first shell came, I was on the second floor of the convent, trying to block the openings of the windows with the remains of bombed blinds, because the gusts of wind had torn my new cloth windows. The second shell fell just in front of me in the Dehaenes' shed. It would be difficult for me to tell you how many times I started to get down. In an instant I found myself outside the door of the kitchen, pale and trembling, holding my hammer in one hand and my bag of nails in the other! . . . 'It's nothing, Sister Marguerite,' said Sister Antoinette, laughing. 'You are still alive!' I thanked the good Lord and went back up, telling myself that where a shell had already fallen, a second would probably not do so. Reaching the top, I saw that all I had nailed was undone and torn. I had to start over! But my courage faltered; my heart was pounding and I still had a headache from the board that had fallen on me on Monday. The work was no longer progressing, it was my poor thumb that received most of the hammer blows destined for the nails. I was forced, therefore, to leave the work for another day. – The house adjoining the riding school was destroyed by a shell. One also fell on Zaalhof, rue de Lille, and on the exercise range where two soldiers were killed and three wounded.

17 DECEMBER – The night was disturbed only by the collapse of a few crumbling walls. Some shrapnel burst on the Welfare School during the day. The cannon continued to thunder and the guns crackled. It seems as though the noise is getting closer. Some shells fell on the Kruistraat and on the commercial district, causing great damage to homes. A doctor from the Friends Unit came to collect me to visit some sick people, because the Sacré Coeur hospital is reserved exclusively for the injured. With the exception of Mr. Van Robaeys there are no more doctors in the city. The Quakers visit all the patients who request it, free of charge, and give them free medicines, even accompanied by donations of money, clothing, food, as they deem necessary. Their charity, generosity and honesty are admirable! At all times and for all, rich or poor, they are ready to sacrifice themselves. Dr. Van Robaeys is also of unfailing dedication, always there during the worst of times and caring nothing of the danger. Dr. Van Robaeys was one of those who had stayed the longest in Ypres and has done much good. May God reward him! – Evening, cannons, rifles and machine guns made a chorus. This is

the fifth day of the furious French attack, but it has not managed to dislodge the Germans from their fortress.

19 DECEMBER – Other than the noise of the guns, everything is pretty quiet: a few shells and shrapnel in the direction of the Welfare School and the station. Thank God! No new dead or injured! Those who can, come to be treated. Thirty-two dressings were done before the arrival of Dr. Fox. I was cobbler tonight, I mended the shoes of Mr. Roose, the vicar.

20 DECEMBER – Only some shrapnel bombs. Three cows were killed. A wounded young man arrived to be treated; his arm terribly swollen and no doctor! They'd just gone out! With a hook, I managed to remove a piece of shrapnel. The poor boy fainted; he must have suffered a lot. After half an hour he was able to head back home. He will return tomorrow. – Later in the day, a few more shrapnel bombs. Towards evening the cannon roared so loudly and so continuously that we could not distinguish the sound of the launch of the shells from that of their landing. The Allies, we are told, want to take a German strong-point. This evening, the bombing of the Sacré Coeur Hospital, where the French had installed a military ambulance unit. The Quakers took their sick and wounded to the cellars.

21 DECEMBER – In the morning, during the early hours, fifty shells fell on the Sacré Coeur. The beautiful chapel is already nothing but a heap of ruins. A number of wounded were transported to La Panne to be received at the Queen's Hospital.[19] The damage is enormous and, what is worse, several French soldiers were wounded and seven were killed, as well as civilians with the Quakers' ambulance, including Raphael Vander Ghote and his companion. The vicar, Gallens, and Gustave Delahaye are also slightly injured. All sick and wounded have been taken to the cellars. It has become obvious that the Germans were again aiming at Red Cross hospitals.

22 DECEMBER – Night and day similar to the previous. A few shells and shrapnel. The Friends will move their hospital to the Lunatic Asylum, rue Thourout. It is Dr. Fox who runs this establishment. It was not to be a long stay, as no sooner than the Sisters had cleaned up and put everything in order, they were forced to return.[20]

23 DECEMBER – Quiet night. Some shrapnel during the day. Mr. Masselein of Potyse who had come to the city to buy bread, was mortally wounded near the station. He was carried into Lagrand's

stable, where he died. Shrapnel burst through the roof of the chemist, Vandenplasse-Samyn, and of the Vandelanoitte residence.

24 DECEMBER – No way to sleep a wink this night: the guns were making too big an uproar. Shrapnel during the day. Many dressings to do. Ed. Deleu's chin is almost healed. Visits to the sick in the city and surroundings. The doctor, though a Protestant, conscientiously warns us when a patient is in danger of dying. It is the parish priest or Mr. Roose, the vicar, who administer the last rites or who are notified, when there is a great distance to cover. Furious gunfire in the evening until about 10 o'clock. – Today I had the opportunity to display my talent as barber, shaving the tonsure of Mr. Roose, the vicar, for the Christmas festivities. The parish priest, who did not find me too inexpert, was my second client! So, another trade, after those of carpenter, fireman, barber, cobbler! What will yet become of me?

25 DECEMBER – During the Mass celebrated by the parish priest, around half past 6, the whistle and explosion of shrapnel and shells began again. The church, that was full of people, emptied in an instant. A woman was killed, rue Bruges; several other people were injured. It is always the same, two injured are healed, three others replace them. The macabre music was repeated from time to time during the day, but more violently towards noon: twice Sister Marie fled into the cellar with her plate. There was a still greater recrudescence around half past 5 – to 6 o'clock. Sad Christmas! If only the child of Bethlehem would bring us peace, He who came to bring it to the earth! – They say that the French and German trenches toward Zillebeke are only 15 metres away from each other!

26 DECEMBER – The night was quite quiet, but more than sixteen shells fell on the Kruisstraat followed by rue Menin and then in the centre of the city. The Muylle home in the Old Clothes Market, among others, has been knocked down. A British soldier was wounded.

27 DECEMBER – Impossible to rest: the French artillery made an infernal noise. Around 7 o'clock, the noise became maddening; the ground shook. In the morning, I went with one of the Quaker doctors to the hamlets of Het Wieltje and Brijke, from where we could see the bombardment of the city. On returning, we learned that, of the shells that fell, Geldhof's kitchen, rue Tuilles, got one; others fell near Saint-Pierre, rue Dixmude and close to the barracks. – In the evening, we

celebrated the Day of the Holy Innocents.[21] Sister Antoinette, the youngest, was named Mother Superior. We had a lot of fun with our new Mother Superior.[22]

28 DECEMBER – A fairly quiet night. During the day, some shrapnel and small shells, especially towards rue Menin. A shell fell right behind our car. Our driver made his machine fly! – In the evening there was continuous lightning!

29 DECEMBER – The wind has caused quite a lot of damage overnight. The cannon thunder is not so loud, the explosions are fewer. However, several people from rue Elverdinghe are injured.

30 DECEMBER – All is quiet. The Germans have lost 1,500 metres. When will we push them back to the borders? Only God knows! The fortress of Zillebeke has fallen: another loss for the Germans. – An English ambulance car took the parish priest, Sister Livine and Sister Marie Berchmans to Poperinghe and Proven, to take New Year wishes to the dean, Rev. Debrouwer, the Superior of the Soeurs Noires and to our own dear Reverend Mother and our Sisters.

31 DECEMBER – Last day of the year! Some shrapnel, but few fell on the city. Later in the day, a few shells fell on the Kruisstraat and the exercise field. A man was injured. The bombing lasted until midnight, and then suddenly everything became calm. Ah! If only this calm could last!

NEW YEAR 1915

1 JANUARY – First Friday of the year! Many citizens of Ypres have returned. The small church of the Soeurs Noires was too small to contain the crowd and the infirmary doors were opened to provide room for those attending. Almost all took Communion. I improvised as police officer to survey the back of the church. – The 'Kaiser', will he send us a New Year's bonus? I fear he will! For the most part, the *marmites* and shrapnel bombs that were launched did not reach the city. It was not until the afternoon, around 3 o'clock, the time of Salvation, that five or six shrapnel bombs burst over our heads with a tremendous noise. One could not hear the parish priest's prelude to the rosary. The attendees, scared, did not know whether to flee or stay. I positioned myself near the small portal in order to leave unnoticed, if necessary. It was not long before Sister Marie Berchamns came for me to dress three wounded. Meanwhile, the Salvation was terminated when one of the patients told us that

other people in the rue des Boudeurs had sustained serious injuries. The priest hastened thither. He found Emma D'Hondt, a girl of 21 years of age, dying. She had been at the Communion Table that morning. The priest gave her the Holy Unction, and brought her in a cart to the convent, where she died a few minutes later, holding in her hands the holy candle and praying, without so much as a complaint. Holy and edifying death. Miss Cloostermans had gone to notify the Friends to take the seriously wounded. – They brought us Marie Dehollander, 17. A small ball of lead had pierced her body just below the right shoulder blade. At the same moment Valentine Woets, 20, entered, crying and shouting, she had her arm smashed above the elbow with small lead balls; a small piece of metal was lodged there. – Miss Cloostermans returned: the ambulance cars of the Friends Unit had gone to another side of the city, in search of the wounded. She went to a French aid station to see if it could bring us help. The parish priest brought in Mrs. Dehollander: a terrible wound in the lower abdomen.

A French medical-major arrived, accompanied by a veterinarian. Together they tended the patient who will be taken with her daughter, Marie, and Valentine Woets to the hospital of the Quakers, who had arrived at that moment. – The two French majors wanted to see the girl who had just died. They could not believe that an injury so light could have taken her. I undressed her, but no other wounds were found. They therefore supposed that the bullet had entered by the chin into the throat and the blood had choked the poor child. – These gentlemen assured us that they were at our service to help us at all times. Terrible afternoon! The Kaiser continues to send us pralines as a Christmas bonus! . . .

2 JANUARY – I was on call at home during the 6 o'clock mass. At around 6 o'clock to half past 6, Mr. Lams arrived with the hearse to seek the dead. – He rang, and I ran to open the door of the room for him, the one that gives onto rue Wenninck, and when turning past the gallery, I hit a stretcher. My candle went out and I could not distinguish the obstacle, but then there came a stench. Groping my way, I found the door. As soon as Mr. Lams went out, I turned to see what had obstructed my way. – It was the body of an old woman, a refugee from Zonnebeke, who had died a miserable death in an attic in the rue des Trèfles. The old woman was already in a state bordering on putrefaction. Sister Berchmans had deposited the body in the gallery and, overloaded with work, forgot to warn me. I had to go back through this gallery during the day and I assure you that it was not without a slight feeling of horror that I looked, from the

corner of my eye, at that which I had so sweetly embraced that morning. Finally, we rolled her in a blanket. – Quiet day: only two shells and they did not explode. I saw a few patients with Dr. Smerdon [of Fau].

3 JANUARY – The cannons broke the windows, and tore the rags that had been used to fill the openings. The guns also caused a disturbance, despite the bad weather. Many people in the church. Mrs. Dehollander died in the Sacré Coeur. During the Salutation I was in my usual place, near the entrance, where Fr. Allemon, from Poperinghe, came to tap me on the shoulder. He arrived in Ypres with two French officers who asked where commander of the de La Croix of the 114th division was buried. As they did not know the way, I accompanied them. Once there, one of the officers seemed deeply moved, and tears escaped from his eyes. I took the liberty of asking him if he knew the deceased personally and he replied that it was his brother. He asked me to look after the grave and tried to give me sixty francs to place a stone on it. I told him to leave that task to the parish priest, which he did. The priest then instructed Mr. Emile Verhack to put the stone in place as soon as possible. For the few francs that remained, the priest gave a service for the soul of the deceased commander.

In the evening, I met a poor French soldier who had come from the trenches, dirty and leaning on a stick. He had frozen feet. I asked him if I could be useful. 'Oh,' he said, 'if you could point me to a French station!' 'There's one opposite us.' He accompanied me and I gave him some clothes, which allowed him to wash those he was wearing. While they were drying, he felt marvelous in the old breeches of an English officer, with a chef's jacket to complete his outfit.

4 JANUARY – Quiet night. Calm day. Some explosions in the distance. The Germans were forced back. It is said that French troops will replace the English. So our good ambulance men will leave us! And what will we do without them? Today, the Quakers sent seven boxes of Bovril and dried peas for our poor and our patients. The parish priest will do his best to keep them here. A few days ago commandant Young brought us two large bags of shirts, and they were welcome! The needs are so great! Now at least we can give some changes of clothing, although we are sometimes forced to give women shirts for men. But war is war! There are many soldiers who have to be content.

Since November 1914, the Friends' Ambulance Unit (FAU) had been involved in the systematic distribution of food and clothing, with distribution depots being established in towns and villages around Woesten, Ypres, Poperinghe and Caestre and over the border in French territory. Many thousands of garments were distributed – most provided through the generosity of Friends in Britain. Friends' Working Parties sprang up all over England and Ireland, with additional help afforded by Red Cross sewing parties, and various war relief societies. Dublin Friends alone contributed over 5,000 articles, and large shipments were received from Friends as far away as America and Canada.

5 JANUARY – The lull appears to continue. Two or three shrapnel only in the meadows near the Lille Gate. – A policeman who was imprudent enough to open a shell was blown to pieces. Another policeman was seriously wounded. The parish priest and doctor Fox had him carried to the Sacré Coeur.

All members of the Committee were present at the meeting today. This association has already done much good and had taken several useful measures. The parish priest read a petition in which he insisted that the Friends Ambulance Unit be able to continue its work of dedication to our city and the surrounding area. Mr. Mayor will be responsible for sending it to the Minister, in Le Havre. The parish priest also requested that relief be organized for the poor, sick and elderly to provide them with soup and milk. Instantly, the first funds, seventy-two francs, were collected from among the Committee members. Measures were also taken to ensure its even distribution, which will start tomorrow. The big *marmite* is on display. In the morning, before doing dressings, the soup will be on the stove to be taken to homes around noon. Sister Marie will boil the milk that will be poured into one litre bottles. Miss Matilda Maroy will help us to take them along with the soup. A list is compiled from the information given by the parish priest, containing names and addresses of those concerned: two families, rue des Chiens; three, rue de Crapaudière; eight Coeur des Veuves; seven, rue des Boudeurs; five, rue Grimminck; five, rue du Canon; three, the Zaalhof; two, rue des Trèfles; five, rue Basse; three, rue de Lille.

Since the parish priest has been staying with us, two watchmen have been spending the nights in his basement. They are Joseph Cottonier and Emile Cilor. This evening, at half past 7, we were at dinner, when one of the two men came to tell us that there were thieves in the priest's home. The priest went there; I followed, equipped with a small lantern. In effect, we found evidence of the looters who must have been surprised in their work, because some bottles of wine had been placed upright and one was uncorked. The jars of jam had all been examined; soap was scattered on the floor; the scale and the candle were still there. The opened bottle was taken away and served to celebrate the eve of the Three Kings. Madame Roose, the queen of the fiesta, went for a Kings' cake.[23]

6 JANUARY – Quiet day. Some cannon shots and some shrapnel out of town, towards the rue Dickebusch, where, we are told, the English are coming back to Ypres. In the evening, around 5 am, three soldiers, undoubtedly the thieves from the day before, were caught stealing wine from the cellar. They had with them a firefighters' cart and they fled through the Lille Gate. Joseph Cottenier wanted to follow them, but was stopped at the door, even though he confirmed that they were the thieves.

7 JANUARY – For a few days I have visited the sick with Dr. Smerdon. Today he brought his replacement, Dr. Thompson. The parish priest usually accompanied the doctor, but he feels it necessary to keep within reach of those who need his spiritual help during these days of continuous bombardment. All patients who give their address to our convent in the rue de Lille are visited for free by the doctors of the Quaker ambulance. Patients who come to the convent, rue de Lille, between 9 o'clock and 10 o'clock, also receive free care from doctors Manning, Fox and Malabar. My chief mission is to serve as guide and interpreter and also to decide which of the sick should be taken to the hospital, which was not always easy! When patients consent, the family's opposition raises new obstacles and often insulting protests abound, these poor people do not understand that we only want to do them good. Once, an old woman of the rue Lapin even grabbed the coal shovel and poker to hit me. Fortunately the English gentlemen, unfamiliar with the Flemish language, do not understand the delicate terms used to repay their devotion.

A few cases of typhoid fever were reported, especially among refugees.[24] My soup was ready from half past 6 this morning. It simmered all morning. At about half past 7, the injured came to have their dressings done. Around 9 am, I accompanied Doctor Thompson and Miss Cloostermans to assist Dr. Manning.

In the afternoon, after giving 'absolution' in the Béguinage church, the parish priest accompanied the body of the policeman to the town cemetery. This is the first time since the bombing of our city that a priest has been back there. After the ceremony, the priest visited the area military commandant, to talk to him about the organization of a hospital for typhoid cases. He promised to undertake the task immediately. Meanwhile, a medical and pharmaceutical service will be temporarily installed. If the priest can provide a suitable place and Sisters, with the essential materials, attempts will be made to set it up without delay.[25] Around noon, I took the soup to the Coeur des Veuves. Math. Maroy took care of the milk.

I am official cobbler! Sister Antoinette has become my client! I am going to mend her shoes.

8 JANUARY – The parish priest, together with Mr. G. W. Young, is responsible for the organization of the hospital for typhoid cases that is to open in the institute of Sacré Ceour. Three Sisters of the Ypres civilian hospital came back with him from Poperinghe. Thus, the number of nuns in the Friends' Ambulance Unit increases.

9 JANUARY – Our good Dean de Brouwer arrived. He looks good, but his priestly heart must bleed upon seeing his beautiful church! What a shame to destroy such artistic gems for no reason! The Dean agreed to eat with us; the Germans appeared to celebrate his return by sending shells. Two French soldiers were killed and five others wounded in Iweins Hall. The house of R. M. Verriest, rue Saint-Jaques, collapsed. Joseph Hoff was injured and came to be attended to immediately. His face is riddled with small particles of metal. With great difficulty, I managed to extract twenty. The parish priest went to inform the military commandant that ten beds were available for typhoid patients. – Evening calm.

10 JANUARY – Some shells. One soldier killed in the barracks. The parish priest reminded the area military commandant that the Friends Ambulance Unit is awaiting permission for it to stay in Ypres. Another shell on H. Pinte's house.

11 JANUARY – The whistlers began at 8 o'clock in the morning and continued until 5 o'clock in the afternoon. In taking the soup, at noon, my five cans and I ran into many dangers! Thankfully, an open door lent us shelter when needed. Just as we got back, some-one came to ask for help for three wounded. Miss Cloostermans has gone to Havre for five days. At N° 8 rue Boudeurs, the little Lacroix-Sinnaeve girl had a serious head injury and the mother, Pharailde Sinnaeve, a wound to the forehead. With temporary bandages in place, they waited for the surgeon to sew the wounds. Ms. Bauwens, a refugee from Zillebeke, in the adjoining house, was in bed with her two-day-old baby, when she was thrown against

the burning stove; the child rolled from its cradle under the bed, but did not suffer the slightest scratch. After dressing several small wounds that the mother had sustained, I ran to warn the ambulance unit. I met the commandant G. W. Young, in a motor car, and we went to collect the wounded to take them both to the Sacré Coeur. Mrs Bauwens had fled with her child, running like a crazy woman, nobody knows where. Two killed and twelve injured in Kruisstraat and a number of damaged houses, including that of the Mahieu family. The Bauwens woman, found in the Kruisstraat, was taken to hospital. – The evening was calm.

12 JANUARY – Around 8 o'clock, three or four small shells came as forerunners. Around 10 o'clock, the parish priest was about to go and visit some parishioners. As he stopped at the door to listen to Mrs. Kerrinkx-Vandevijver, who had come to talk to him, an explosion was heard above us. The hat and cape of the parish priest and my apron sustained several holes. It was an explosive bomb which made a hole right next to the sewer, where I found the head of the shell. We remained unharmed. God be praised. Mrs. Zelie Duprez-Legrand was wounded in the face, hand and leg. I was able to extract seven metal splinters, but an eighth remained and the leg swelled. Fortunately, Dr. Smerdon had come to tend the sick. Having completed his work here, he went with the parish priest to visit patients in their homes. Around noon, shrapnel burst into the treatment room. Today, the Rev. Mr. Roose baptised Florent Verschoore. The ceremony took place in our dining hall. Shrapnel fell on the Didier home, rue de l'Arsenal, mortally wounding Mrs. Dondeyne-Dehollander, her daughter and her step-son, Alyntho.

13 JANUARY – It was only in the evening, around 5 o'clock, that seven or eight shrapnel bombs arrived in succession. One wounded in rue Grimminck. The dean arrived. This time he will remain at the convent where Sister Berchmans has prepared him a bed in the potato cellar, which has already served as home to the parish priest, for weeks.

14 JANUARY – We are living in a very dark cellar. If only, at least, it had been quiet! But no! For 2 ½ hours our sleep was disturbed. We counted eighteen shrapnel. A reliable omen for the day! Indeed, no less than fifty. Only one injured person was brought to us. A new typhoid case was carried to Sacré Coeur. Baptism of André Clinckemaillie in the chapel of our Convent. Miss Cloostermans is the wartime godmother. The dean decided to move to Mrs. Boone's

house (rue de Stuers), since there is no priest on that side of town. He will say Mass at the Pauvres Claires.

15 JANUARY – The small property of C. Bailleul is on fire and several houses in Brielen. The English cannon thundered, while four or five airplanes flew over the town, making the ground shake. The parish priest went to find the helpless old people, so they could be led to a safe place by the Friends.

Sister M. Berchmans and Sister Antoinette went to visit our sick Sister Gabrielle, in Poperinghe. It was only with much difficulty that they managed to get back into Ypres without a pass.

16 JANUARY – Great cannonnade! The parish priest accompanied the first little old woman taken by car to the Pauvres Claires. In passing, he shouted several things to me, that I did not understand, then, suddenly, I saw him fall out of the car. I ran in haste.

He was unconscious. Four French soldiers carried him into the convent. He had a wound next to his left eye, which I dressed. I then washed it with vinegar, but it was only after an hour that he came-to. He was suffering a lot with his left shoulder, and he was unable to dress during the following days. What a sacrifice for him not to make his charitable rounds.

17 JANUARY – The parish priest has had a bad night. In the morning I am going to ask the Reverend Mr. Declercq replace him for Mass at the Soeurs Noires. Monsieur le curé will say it with us. Today, to our delight, we could celebrate the Blessed Sacrament in our chapel for the first time since 10 October.

18 JANUARY – Today it was the Hospice of Saint Jean that would hold the Blessed Sacrament. Mr. Roose celebrated two Masses: one at 6 o'clock and one at 8 o'clock. Mr Declercq said two Masses in the Soeurs Noires and the dean said it in the Pères Carmélites. – Tonight, a British soldier was killed in the Brasserie Vermeulen. The Leupens' house, near Saint-Jaques, was hit. No injuries.

19 JANUARY – Around 5 o'clock in the evening, five or six shells while we spent an hour in adoration before the Blessed Sacrament, in the cellar of the Soeurs Noires.

20 JANUARY – One wounded in the Plain d'Amour. Today, the dean received a mandate from the Cardinal, Monseigneur Vico, conferring upon him episcopal rights. In the evening, terrible cannonnade.

21 JANUARY – Around half past 2 in the morning, some shrapnel. Around 6 in the evening, eight shells. A colonel, a sergeant and six soldiers were killed in a house near the Welfare School, which collapsed. – It rained all day!

22 JANUARY – In the morning, four Taubes came on reconnaissance. A day of bombs. Several wounded and two killed, on the Menin road.

23 JANUARY – The Taubes are back. They continued. They say one fell on Poperinghe. An artillery battle engaged. The dean and the parish priest went to Poperinghe to see Mr. Jules Baus, who holds the letters and papers relating to the Episcopal appointment of the Rev. Mr. Dean Debrouwer. Around half past 8, the bombardment renewed on the Saint Jacques and Kafvaart side. A man was killed on rue Thourout.

24 JANUARY – Quiet day; nothing in particular. Many dressings.

25 JANUARY – Explosions in the evening and at night, especially on the gas plant and Kruistraat. Could it be true that the Germans have suffered heavy losses near Zonnebeke?

26 JANUARY – Members of the Committee addressed a letter to Mr. Young, thanking him for all he has done for the people of Ypres.

The letter was translated into English and published in the Quaker journal, *The Friend*, that carried news about the Friends' Ambulance Unit's activities in France and Belgium, during the war:

Honoured Sir,
The Committee which has been formed in Ypres to replace the Communal Council, which was put to flight by the bombardment of the city, desires to express to you, as well as to the English doctors, and ambulance assistants their profound gratitude for the inestimable services that you have rendered to our unhappy population. Braving all perils you evacuated the almshouses of Nazareth and St. John; conveyed away hundreds of sufferers; visited and tended the sick and wounded at their homes; organized for them a hospital at the Institute of the Sacred Heart, and effected their safe deliverance during the bombardment of the building. You have also installed a

service of ambulances. You perform your charitable labour with perfect courtesy, a noble generosity, and the most complete disinterestedness and self-sacrifice.

From our hearts our Committee thanks you, and begs you to accept the assurance of its distinguished esteem.[26]

Two explosions at night and another two around noon. Today, Commander G. W. Young accompanied the parish priest to the meeting of the Committee and he proposes:

1. to disinfect water from the ramparts and to place barrels of sterilized water for the use of residents;
2. to inspect milk and beer;
3. to give antityphoid injections. We see many cases of typhoid fever, especially among refugees. – Efforts will be made to evacuate them.[27]

27 JANUARY – Notice is given that, on the occasion of the anniversary of the Kaiser, the Germans are preparing to send us marmites stuffed with 'pralines'. The cannons were quite noisy, but it was the Allies who gratified the Germans with some 'sweets'. Around noon, however, three or four exploding shells landed on the casements. – Mr. G. W. Young bought many barrels from Vandenbogaerde's and taps from M. Vanhee. Camille D'Haene is responsible for filling them and placing them where indicated. – Burial of Ms. Devos, from the Post Office.

28 JANUARY – About noon, three or four shrapnel injuring five people, rue Elverdinghe and rue Saint-Jean. When I arrived to give help, one of the Quakers' ambulances was already there, taking the two most seriously injured; I dressed the other three, to whom I promised that I would go each day to renew the dressings, because these poor people were afraid even to cross the street.

The Friends are placing disinfected water barrels: at the Lille Gate, Menin Gate, in the barracks and the Saint-Jaques casements. Mr. G. W. Young proposed to the priest the creation of a 'Search Party' to seek out the typhoid cases. This great work was entrusted to Mr. A. R. Baker, after which Mr. G. W. Young returned to England to spend a few days of well deserved rest.

It was of crucial importance to the military authorities to ascertain the state of health of the local civilian population with which the troops were likely to come into contact. Cases of contagious disease could thus be isolated, and appropriate treatments administered. It was to this end that the Friends' Ambulance Unit created the 'Search Party' in February 1915, at the height of the typhoid epidemic in the Ypres area. Its job was to discover and remove to hospital all those typhoid cases that had either been undetected or simply undisclosed to the authorities. This involved systematic and painstaking house-to-house searches beginning in Ypres and later extending to neighbouring villages. The work was sanctioned by the Belgian Minister of the Interior, who bestowed upon the Unit the power to carry out such evacuation.

The Search Party consisted of four FAU orderlies and four interpreters (usually nuns who could speak both Flemish and French) who worked in pairs. The teams were taken to the area in question by ambulance, then collected at the end of the day, after carrying out the search on foot.

With the aid of the interpreter, the orderly questioned the occupants of each house, as to whether there was any illness among them. All information gleaned from the interviews was recorded on a card together with the address of the house and the number and names of occupants. The source of the home's water supply and the state of its sanitation were also noted, as well as whether troops had been billeted in the house or whether they had been sold milk, butter or beer. Those individuals not already inoculated against typhoid were encouraged to attend the centres where this would be carried out. Finally, enquiry was made as to the nature of any assistance required.

29 JANUARY – At night, a few explosions in the distance. In the city, the sky remains calm. Some shells in the flooded plains.[28] Mr. A. R. Baker came to the convent with a few gentlemen of the Quakers to finalize how to organize the 'Search Party'. This is how we are to operate: Every day from 9 o'clock to 12 o'clock in the morning and 2 o'clock to 4 o'clock in the afternoon, all the houses, cellars, attics and casements will be visited, first in the centre of the city and then the surrounding area, and Poperinghe. Today, two Doctors of the Friends and five assistants arrived at the convent, rue de Lille. Doctor Manning will stay in the sewing room to do dressings with Miss Cloostermans, who will, at the same time, act as interpreter to him. Assistants, Mr. Tallerman and Mr. Wallice will give anti-typhoid inoculations in our refectory.[29] Other assistants will go with the 'Search Party', each with a Sister as an interpreter. Sister Lucia, of the Soeurs Noires, will accompany Mr. Geoff Thompson; Sister Margaret of the Providence, Mr. J. Jennings, and Sister Estelle, St. Joseph's School, Mr. Harris. I will go with Mr. Robert Stopford. In our ambulance service, as drivers, we have Mr.

Littleboy, Mr. J. Locke, Dr. Fox or Dr. Thompson who will join in, one or the other, depending on the circumstances.

In each family, the state of health was checked and, if necessary, the sick removed. Ways were also sought to help the old people and children to leave the city. The Friends assisted the needy by giving them money, or clothing, and food. Milk was checked. The latrines and water deposits were also examined and disinfectants provided when necessary, etc.

Infected houses are marked:

X yellow: typhoid cases not evacuated.

V_____ taken to hospital but not yet disinfected.

X blue: dyphtheria.

X red: scarlet fever.

A soldier of the Red Cross R.A.M.C. followed us to carry out the disinfection.

It was forbidden for soldiers to enter the marked houses, either to shop or to do their laundry there.

Where there was need to burn the beds and bedding, those affected were handed a card, with which they had to come straight to us to get a new bed plus the accessories.

The system of markings described by Soeur Marguerite does not coincide exactly with that recorded by the Friends' Ambulance Unit.[30] According to the official history of the FAU, those houses in which a suspected case was discovered had a 'V' painted on the door. When the patient was removed this V was converted into an X by the driver of the ambulance. These painted marks served as a guide to the Sanitary Section of the London Territorial Division, who, acting on information supplied from the cards, carried out the necessary disinfection of houses from which cases had been removed. When this had been done, a ring of yellow was painted round the X previously painted on the door. The disinfection of belongings such as clothing, bedding and mattresses was also carried out. People who had to have their possessions taken away for disinfection were given a card noting the articles in question and their time of collection as Soeur Marie indicates. Those whose mattress had to be burned were given a similar token which authorized them to pick up a new on from the Convent St Marie or other designated station.

On the evening of the 29th, a few exploding shells fell in the city, including one in Laroy's stable; one on Mr. J. Baus's greenhouse, and one in Mr. Angillis's kitchen; there were no injuries.

The English came in search of a place to stay for two hundred and fifty soldiers in need of rest. Oh! The brave men!

30 JANUARY – At night, between 12 and 1 o'clock, fifteen bombs. In the afternoon, some shrapnel bombs. Mrs. Vandamme, who was going to the Sacré Coeur with her newborn child to be baptized, was mortally wounded; Mr. Callens, the vicar, who was close by, attended immediately. Around midnight, a large shrapnel bomb, followed by several *marmites*, on the casements and Saint-Jaques church; fortunately, many fell into the water.

31 JANUARY – In the morning, at 8 o'clock, the cannon roared, and between half past 4 and 6 o'clock, the noise became infernal. The parish priest accompanied Dr. Thompson to visit the sick; a fourth ward for typhoid cases was opened in the Sacré Cœur.

1 FEBRUARY – The new month seemed to be beginning calmly, when, at about half past 4 in the afternoon, six cannons, simultaneously, belched their deadly devices. A number of shrapnel bombs followed, but only two or three exploded. The others fell into the water of the ramparts.[31] At night, heavy artillery prevented us from sleeping. The trenches gained by the Germans, last Friday, were recovered from them again. But they took advantage of this relief to approach the towns near Saint-Eloi, Hollebeke and Zillebeke. They are no more than four kilometres away.

2 FEBRUARY – A British military ambulance has moved into the Saint Jean hospice. In the evening the first three wounded and one old soldier were taken there. The celebration of the Virgin Saint passed peacefully. – The doctors of the Friends' Ambulance Unit began injections against typhoid fever. The parish priest, the Abbot Declercq and the lawyer, Mr. Reynaert, were the first inoculated. Towards evening, Dr. Smerdon came to inject us in the convent.

In addition to the other measures of disease prevention put in place by the FAU, at the request of the British 2nd Army, it also undertook the task of inoculating the civil population of Ypres and surrounding districts, opening inoculation stations in schools, convents and other buildings, where its doctors would carry out the vaccination of all those who attended. In addition, many people were visited in their own homes. Those carrying out the Search Party work also promoted the inoculation scheme, explaining to those they visited the crucial importance of being vaccinated, as well as informing them of the whereabouts of the nearest station and the times and days that it would be carried out. This information was repeated in notices in French and Flemish posted around the town. Inoculation was not made obligatory by the Belgian Government until April 1915, and the FAU volunteers had to use all their powers of persuasion to induce the locals to subject themselves to it voluntarily. Nevertheless, thanks to the help of the local priest, Delaere, and Soeur Marguerite and her fellow nuns, the campaign proved very successful. The FAU was eventually operating eleven inoculation stations in Ypres and the scheme was subsequently extended to the surrounding towns and villages.

3 FEBRUARY – The night is calm, and also the day, thankfully, as everyone is a little out-of-sorts effect of inoculation. A Taube dropped three bombs. The Countess Louise d'Ursel honors us with a visit. More than two hundred soldiers, with their officer, have come to stay at the convent. Our poor soldiers found tanks full of water to wash themselves. They needed to get out of the trenches, I assure you! The boards and the wings of the theatre will serve as beds. It will always be less damp than the bare ground!

4 FEBRUARY – The 'Search Party' did good work, despite the shrapnel and shells. Rue Corte du Marais, two people killed. Bombs on Gruwez, in front of the barracks; rue des Aveugles, on housing; rue des Trèfles, on the Vandenbulcke home, on the mess and the dining room, Fripont, where dinner was waiting for the officers, who fortunately had not yet made their entrance. – In Nazareth, in the barracks, in the Manège, rue des Tuiles, all over the Saint-Pierre district, the English ambulances were installed. Everything was carried out under this rain of shrapnel and shells. A bad night is feared. Some German airplanes came on reconnaissance.

5 FEBRUARY – Bad night, indeed! Several shrapnel around half past 10. Forty-five minutes later, a shell exploded in our chapel, destroying part of the roof shingles. The benches were broken, the hearth and the walls were perforated, the throne of the Holy Virgin knocked down, while the figure remained standing, intact! Several doors and windows fixed, as well as possible, at the cost of fifteen working days, during my free time, were entirely blown away; two stations of the Cross are damaged; the statue of the Infant Jesus of Prague, blown off its pedestal, is standing intact in the middle of the chapel, in front of a large hole in the ground. The tabernacle is smashed; the Sacred Hosts were scattered on the altar. The parish priest picked them up and carried them into the sacristy, together

with the figure of Our Lady of Thuyne that was above the altar. She had been turned, and a piece of the crown blown off. Everyone returned to the cellar, but at one o'clock someone came to ask us for help. A house in the street of the Prison had collapsed; the husband and wife Muyelle-Pinet were in the rubble. Miss Cloostermans ran there first, but came back immediately: the two victims had undoubtedly been killed instantly. We had a great deal of trouble removing the bodies in the darkness. The bed in which they had been resting was left hanging between heaven and earth.

In the morning we were brought the news that the Chapel of the Sœurs Noires had also been bombed. The shell, that had entered on the garden side, made a small hole on the outside, then, passing under the foundations, had made a large cavity in the interior and had broken many valuable items. Impossible to carry on saying the Sainted Mass there. So, we are following the parish priest to St. Godelieve. Sister Livine and Sister Antoinette used the day to arrange the chapel of the Sœurs Noires as best they could, to celebrate Mass tomorrow.

During the day, shrapnel here and there; several 'Taubes' came to watch over the city. One of them dropped a firebomb on the Costeur home, rue de Lille, a few metres from me. The English who were with us ran to smother the fire and returned, happily, with parts of the device. The English, they say, have recovered four trenches lost by the French.

In the afternoon, the parish priest handed me the keys to the *Chapelle des Ames du Purgatoire* telling me to go to the church to chase thieves. I went with a soldier who was staying with us. We found two soldiers of the North Somerset Camp trying to open the tomb of St. Anthony. When I entered, they looked at me intently, like naughty children caught in the act. I did not need to talk to them; they retreated, eyes downcast.

Upon returning to the convent, I met the engineer Mr. Vander Ghote. While I was talking to him, I was struck by the appearance of a large dog. I pointed out that every day about the same time, the same dog was there, seeming to come from Sant Jacques and heading for the Lille Gate; the fact had been noticed by several people for six weeks. Was it a German dog? The case was brought to the attention of two or three officers and, after a few days, the dog appeared no more.

6 FEBRUARY – Night and day quiet. – Two trenches taken by the British. The cannon made big a row.

7 FEBRUARY – One would think that the war was over, it is so quiet. Can the Germans have lost another 5 kilometres of land? Reawakening of cannon, gunfire, shrapnel bombs into the evening and night. – A soldier-priest who celebrated Mass in the church Elverdinghe was seriously injured in front of the altar.

The Sacré Coeur hospital is filling more and more. It has 470 sick and 134 serious surgery cases. In addition, thousands of people receive care, dressings, consultations and other aid from the doctors of the Friends' Ambulance Unit, all for free.[32]

8 FEBRUARY – Night and morning calm. In the afternoon, the Germans sent explosive bombs. They fell, above all, on the Welfare School, the Kruisstraat and the château Ansette. – Sister Marie Antoinette and Marie Vanuxem are organising a class in the basement of our nursery school. It will open tomorrow.

9 FEBRUARY – At noon, while taking food to the Cour de Veuves, an exploding bomb forced me to lie almost flat to escape the shrapnel. That same day, Mr. Vienea was injured by large stones thrown by a shell in front of the Saint-Pierre church.

10 FEBRUARY – Bombing resumed at 7 o'clock. The shells came one after the other. Two bombs were dropped by a Taube in the rue des Chiens, on the Vermeulen home, near me, while I was running with my soup for the poor who were waiting for me at the nursery school; the second bomb fell in the garden of Mr. Lepergue, rue du Lombard. Thank God! No new injuries! – Someone warned us that thick smoke was coming out of our chimney. We made sure of the cause: it was simply the soot that was inflamed. More shrapnel bombs over the city. The Taubes were put to flight by the English and two were hit before the evening.

11 FEBRUARY – A shower of shells towards the Kruisstraat and the exercise field half past one to 2 o'clock and half past 3 to half past 4. A house collapsed: five killed. A man is seriously injured in Château-d'Eau. – A spy was arrested. – A soldier was shot in the barracks. Around half past 8, at bedtime, shells fell around our area, two in St. Godelieve, one in the casements, one on Maurice Desramault's house, one on Céline Geysen's, one on the Saint-Louis schoolroom, one on the Mahieu shop, etc.

At that moment, an ambulance car was taking four wounded to the Soeurs of Godelieve; a bomb killed the two stretcher-bearers and their four patients. They brought us Arthur Dehaene, seriously injured, Charles Dehaene and one of the Maertens children. – This day was full of sad incidents. A woman brought us a young baby to tend to, thinking it was hers. Upon arriving at the convent she realized that it was Charles Dehaene's child. And her child! What had become of it? Poor mother! Eight were found dead near the casements. The parish priest gave them all conditional Extreme Unction. They were: Charles Dehaene, died on the way to us, and his wife; Alixe Vandenberghe's wife and two children. Hof. Dubois's wife and their two daughters, Madeleine (12 years old) and a second child, 9 years old. The men came out of the casements to give assistance. The corpses were deposited with us in the covered courtyard. Miss Cloostermans went to the Sacré Coeur to get help and waited for it to come. I carried the little Dehaene boy, who had an arm and a leg broken. It was only then that, to my surprise, I noticed that I was ready for bed, without stockings and in slippers. They gave me two blankets to cover myself and took me quickly back to the convent. The next morning, before the arrival of soldiers, and in the presence of family members, we went through the victims' pockets to give their relatives whatever they might contain. Then Sister Livine and I carried them to the Soeurs Noires where they were wrapped in blankets. – The little ones, Dehaene and Maertens, died in hospital. Six soldiers were killed in the home of Maurice Desramault, four others, rue du Lombard. Many were injured and were taken to Saint Jean, where six of them died a few hours later.

It is said that these bombs were launched over the city from a German armoured vehicle. The British blew up the railway lines, to prevent a repetition of such massacres.

12 FEBRUARY – The day passed quietly.

13 FEBRUARY – At 8 o'clock, funeral service. The eight victims were contained in five coffins. The church of the Soeurs Noires was too small for the crowds. Heartbreaking ceremony. I was especially sensitive this morning, as this was the third time we had buried one of my students. – Two hundred and fifty Scottish soldiers will lodge with us and two hundred and fifty in our nursery school.

14 FEBRUARY – Nothing in particular. – A policeman was killed in rue de Lille. – The English have retaken two trenches.

15 FEBRUARY – 152 people came to be injected. Since 28 January, 11,000 have been inoculated for the first time and 10,000 for the second time. The cases of typhus are gradually diminishing. The

civilians in the city consume about 65,000 litres of disinfected water, daily. This task is carried out under the control of an R.A.M.C. captain and the engineer W. Buckton, of the Quakers. – The pool of the Swimming School, now in military use, was also disinfected. Mr. Donald Gray controls the water in the barrels for civilian use. A box of chloride and written instructions showing how to use it are given to those who live far from the centre. We distributed to over 5,000 families.

The first bombardment of Ypres in November 1914 had destroyed the town's water supply – to the great detriment of the health of the local population. People were obliged to draw water from the stagnant moat surrounding the town, from disused wells and underground rain-water tanks – some of which were in dangerously close proximity to sewers that had also been damaged by bombardment. It would not be long before cases of enteric fever and related diseases appeared.

When the British Army took up occupation of the region, sanitary teams set about improving conditions in the area where troops were to be stationed. Particular attention was paid to the water supply. With the assistance of Captain Coplans of the RAMC and W. W. Buckton of the BRCS, the FAU was entrusted by the British military authorities to organise a civilian supply of chemically-treated drinking water in and around Ypres. Technical assistance was provided by the Belgian Civil Engineer, Mr Vanderghote, and 19 local labourers were employed to carry out the work at the pumping stations that were set up. Several pumps and large barrels of 50 and 130 gallons capacity were purchased and stationed at convenient points in the town. Water was pumped into the barrels and treated with chloride of lime – this chlorinated water then being made available to the civilian population. A separate supply for troops was organised by the military authorities.

Under the direction of Geoffrey Young, the FAU had posters and leaflets printed warning members of the public of the dangers arising from the consumption of impure water, and informing them of the new facilities for obtaining a chemically-treated supply. Householders in more remote or inaccessible areas were issued with small packets of chloride of lime. A small metal measuring spoon was also provided, together with clear instructions, in both French and Flemish, as to how to carry out the purification of the water.

Civilians were initially reluctant to drink the treated water, because of its rather bitter taste and cloudy appearance, but with the aid of father Delaere, Soeur Marguerite and the nuns, Geoffrey Young and his men convinced people of the absolute necessity of this measure. The instructions read as follows:

Instructions for using the disinfectant powder
With the little spoon attached to the card, measure a good spoonful of powder and mix it with 15 litres of water.
Let the water stand for half an hour before using it.
This specially prepared powder being very strong, a half spoonful is quite sufficient for a bucket or a large jug. Use only the little spoon attached.
The powder should be kept in a hermetically sealed box.
It is very dangerous to drink water or to use it for washing plates and dishes without disinfecting it according to these instructions.

16 FEBRUARY – Quiet in the centre, but along the Kammel road, many houses were destroyed.

An army captain, sent by Mr. G. W. Young, came to find the parish priest to take action with respect to the soldiers' laundry. So far, the first-comers were attended to first, which had many drawbacks: often the washing was not ready when they had to return to the trenches or to move out; other times items were lost or exchanged. Hence, there were disputes between civilians and soldiers. The parish priest has been made responsible for the organization. He sent me to find twelve laundry women, who will be at the infantry barracks from 8 o'clock, tomorrow morning.

The following conditions have been set:

1. The workers must be married women;
2. They will talk to me with regard to the job's requirements;
3. They will enter and leave the barracks empty-handed and with empty pockets;
4. They will receive 4 fr. daily plus lunch;
5. The work will begin at 7 o'clock in the morning and finish at 4 o'clock in the afternoon. Half-an-hour will be given for lunch, at midday;
6. A soldier will be responsible for bringing water. No employee will leave the job without permission from the supervisor who is an English soldier, with bayonet fixed.

17 FEBRUARY – Our new laundry was installed to the sound of cannon, and greeted by a half dozen shrapnel bombs! At around 7 o'clock, the twelve laundry assistants were at the convent, from where I led them to the infantry barracks, which is full of Scottish

soldiers. A stove full of hot water awaited them, and work was begun without delay. Once the tubs were rinsed and in order, work was good and solid! Ms. Meersman will direct the work and indicate the role of each worker. At around 9 o'clock, I was able return to the convent, where my usual activities were awaiting me. Another very useful improvisation, thanks to the parish priest.

18–19–20 FEBRUARY – Intermittent noise of cannons and showers of shrapnel. The explosions multiplied on the evening of the 20th. It looked like a violent storm.

Dr. Thompson went with me to the Sonneville family to persuade them to let their daughter, Gabrielle, 22, with typhoid fever, go to hospital. Three weeks ago, another daughter Martha (20) was taken there. But the parents have decided, 'no way'! The proposal was met by insults! In truth, we have got used to it. We had to use force and take her anyway! Dr. Thompson, the driver and myself placed the patient on a stretcher and laid her in the auto-ambulance. The poor child was so sick that she was aware of nothing.

It is hard to have to act by force, but it is sometimes necessary in the common interest, as was the case here. When a bombardment was announced, the patient was taken into the casements where she became a danger to the hundreds of people who were there! These rather stringent measures were not general. If the doctor's instructions were followed strictly, patients could remain in the care of their families and, if necessary, we visited the home. But for those who were negligent, especially refugees, they were taken to the hospital. In case of open opposition, which was rare, two gendarmes attended quickly.

21 FEBRUARY – The Germans took two trenches from the Allies that these are now desperate to recover. Bombs and exploding shells played a great part in the fighting, and the British soldiers, who were *en repos* for five days, left in haste to lend a hand to their brothers-in-arms.

22 FEBRUARY – Cannons, rifles, shrapnel bombs formed a chorus! Towards evening, record for bombs! They fell in large numbers in the moat around the ramparts. Each time, there was a column of water 10 metres high and hundreds of fish were thrown onto the banks. – Several men near the hostel 'De Engel' on the Lille road, tried to open a shell that exploded in their hands. Emile Crepeele, single, 36, is in pieces. Thomas Deruddere, a young father, was smashed against a wall. Little Albert Hoornaert was seriously injured. At the news of

the accident, Dr. Manning, Robert Stopford and the driver went to the scene by car. But at the Lille Gate we learned that from 6 o'clock in the morning until 6 o'clock in the evening, the free passage of vehicles is forbidden. I too, was forbidden to pass. The roadway was constantly bombarded, to prevent the passage of troops. So, doctors Manning and Stopford, each with a stretcher, and followed by Mr. Littleboy and Mr. Thompson, went alone to the site of the disaster. Soeur Lucie and I stayed in the car. After half an hour, they returned bringing only little Hoonaert who was horribly wounded all over his body, and was immediately taken to the Sacré Coeur. We resumed the care of the dead in the evening, at 6 o'clock, and we continued our 'Search Party'. Three typhoid cases in the parish of Saint Pierre died today in hospital: Romaine Maertens (13), Emma Meersman (15) and Gabrielle Sonneville (22). As needs increase, so does the dedication of the doctors and Sisters. Today 236 people were inoculated against typhus. A refugee, Cuypers, also fell victim to his own imprudence, in wanting to open a shell. He had made a small business from selling German shells to the English. In the evening, despite the shrapnel, we had to find the two bodies. I armed myself with a lantern and Sister Lucia accompanied me. Four soldiers willingly escorted us, but they had to leave for the trenches. Carrying our lantern and two stretchers, we followed the soldiers, who were taking the same road, fully expecting to meet more soldiers who could help us at the Lille Gate. The people who saw us pass thought that we were going to the battlefield and begged us not to expose ourselves to danger. Near the Lille Gate, we did indeed find soldiers at rest. Four little Scottish men joined in immediately and took charge of the stretchers. But the sentry extinguished our lantern and we had to follow our route in deep darkness, as there was a thick fog. Hundreds of soldiers marched before us and yet a perfect silence reigned. From time to time the rockets that were launched from the trenches threw some light on our way. Reaching our destination, with the aid of a match we could make out the bodies in a bag found in the neighbouring house. The body of Emile Crépeele was literally in pieces: one arm could not be found.

The head and shoulders of Thomas Derrudere remained stuck to the wall, and were so strongly attached that Sister Lucia and I were forced to use our nails to remove them as best we could. We were half-an-hour away from the Soeurs Noires where we had to take the bodies, and though the flares lit up the way quite often, the difficulty of the road, the weight of the burden and the amassing of more than 1,200 soldiers marching to the trenches of Saint-Eloi, and who at each turn received orders to stop, caused our progress to be very slow.

Finally, after an hour and a half of effort, we came to the convent, where the bodies were wrapped in blankets.

23 FEBRUARY – Between 11 o'clock and noon, a shell greeted us and the Dean, who arrived for lunch. Today is the first meeting of Monsigneurs the priests.

24 FEBRUARY – The Dumortier home, Kruisstraat, collapsed. Despite a rain of shells, the 'Search Party' continued. Soon the whole city will have been covered. Tonight we will still have to visit some families to persuade them to send their patients to the hospital.

25 FEBRUARY – The parish priest Delaere will talk to the Dean about the measures to be taken for orphans and the helpless in the town.

For four days the soldiers of the R. B. Hussars, C Squadron, have been *en repos* in our convent. Around noon, as I saw several come out of a bombed area with small packages which they hid under their jackets. I walked over to them to see what they were carrying so preciously. Well! They had found the place where we had hidden the different costumes used for our small theatre performances and each had selected his own! This find has inspired them to organize a concert before heading to the trenches, tomorrow. The games room, bombed, will serve as concert room. These are the corporals who will organize it. The officers and the Sisters and soldiers in the area, are invited. Mr. Gilbert, the brewer, whom I had told about the project, sent a barrel of beer for their disposal. Miss Leys will take care of the sweets. There will be wine for the officers. Towards evening, our troops were doing their usual tour around the city, one wearing a wig, the other with a false beard, others playing the flute, trumpet, cymbals and the drum.

The concert began at about 7 o'clock. The officers were in the place of honor. In turn, the actors appearing on stage were disguised as Chinese, Negroes, quacks, etc. There were musical episodes and songs whose choruses were repeated by the whole room. In short, our brave soldiers were having fun like children, without worrying about the shells falling continuously in our neighbourhood and without thinking that for many of them, perhaps, that day might have no tomorrow.

26 FEBRUARY – All was quiet in the town. Today, the 'Search Party' explored Kruisstraat. When Mr. Stopford and I left house No. 38, a shrapnel bomb burst, then a few steps further on, two shells.

The first ruined a house in the Pannenhuisstraat. We went there with Mr. Harry and Sister Marguerite of Providence, who was in the area at the same time as us. A woman was under the rubble, severely injured. Her one-year-old child was dead at her side and the eight-day-old baby was unscathed. The woman and baby were taken to the Quaker hospital. The second shell had landed 50 metres away, killing two British soldiers and three civilians, including Menu and Lefever, who had returned the evening before from Malassise, Saint-Omer, recovered from typhoid fever. A man had had his hand severed, Lucien Masselin had lost two fingers, others had minor injuries. Two Taubes came to inspect the area.

27 FEBRUARY – Quiet day. Towards evening the parish priest asked me to deliver a letter to rue St Elizabeth. Sister Marie Berchmans was with me. Near the Fraipont house, we saw ten Scottish soldiers standing guard, with fixed bayonets. No trespassing. They said there was a spy on the roof, giving signals to the Germans. He will certainly not escape, because the house is surrounded. But who would venture out onto the roof? The armed officers were most courageous, that goes without saying! Meanwhile, in light of the moon one could see a hand or an arm, or a head moving in different directions. However, the officers returned empty-handed! Well then? The spy? It was simply a flap of canvas nailed to the roof to replace the removed tiles, and the wind was moving it.
We certainly had fun with this adventure!

28 FEBRUARY – With the calm and beautiful weather, two Taubes came to cast their prying eyes on the city; but they were soon followed and hit by the English.
This morning, as I was returning with Mathilde Maroy from the Reverend Fathers, where we had heard the Holy Mass, we witnessed a very touching act from an English soldier. In the rue de Lille, we met several wounded returning from combat. One of these brave men was leading a German, the very one who had wounded him. At the corner of rue Cassel, a woman came running, bringing milk to the injured. But remembering that her husband had been the first victim of German bombs in Ypres, she refused to give this enemy a drink. But the wounded Englishman, having half-emptied his glass, turned and passed the rest to the German. – This is not the first time we have seen such acts of generosity. This reminds me of the day when 400 English and 11 wounded German prisoners arrived at our convent. One of the officers ordered us not to give sweets to the

Germans. But soon after his departure, I saw a sentinel share his ciga-
rettes with them, then he came to ask me for 'some jam' for the
prisoners, which I gave him, with the consent of the Reverend
Mother. That same day, a little German, only 16 years old, was crying
bitterly, in the belief that the English were going to shoot him. I had
great difficulty in making him understand that he would be treated
well by the English.

Towards evening, a dozen shrapnel bombs near the Welfare
School. Rev. Mr. Baelde came to tell the Curé about a refugee family
that is in the greatest distress, the priest ordered Sister Livine and
myself to go to Brielenpoorte. We found the mother who had been
bedridden for three weeks, devoured by fever. Her mouth and teeth
were as black as ink. I enquired of her husband. She replied by signs
that he was at her side. But he was under the bed, from where, with
great difficulty, we got him out, for which he thanked us by spitting
in our faces! He was so ill that the poor man was rambling and angry.
Five small children, dirty and scruffy, like everything else there, were
playing in the same room, the only one in the house. It had a small
recess that served as a granary. They had not eaten all day. The boy
of 11 chopped me some wood to make fire. I prepared soup with
Bovril I had brought, then I prepared meat that Mr. Baelde had given
me for them. Meanwhile, Sister Livine busied herself in the dim light
of our lantern, in washing and refreshing the father. I then put the
little ones to bed. Poor bed! Five or six soldiers' jackets spread out in
a corner of the room, and to cover it a blanket and two more jackets.
It was then the turn of the mother to be washed and refreshed, but
she was so weak that one alone would not suffice for the task. The
next day, the 'Friends' car came to take away the two patients.
Thanks to the generous interest of Dean Debrouwer, the care of the
children was entrusted to a woman from the neighbourhood. From
time to time, either he or I went to visit. After a few days, we had to
take two of the boys to the hospital. When they arrived there, father
and mother had already passed into the next life. The Curé will take
care of children in the future.

1 MARCH – Five or six shrapnel bombs burst on the civil cemetery, several others on Kruisstraat. The Count of Beaumont and Mr.
Chopard came today to offer the parish priest a castle in Normandy
for the orphans of Ypres and surroundings. A beautiful deed that the
parish priest had long dreamed of. The orphans! He lacks nothing,
but the rest! Come on! Soon it will be done.

Despite the snow, rain and wind, the 'Search Party' made its
explorations. Here, I must recount a striking feature of providential

protection, of which Mr. Stopford and I were the subjects, today. In a small cellar under the butchers' market, where we were surprised by a downpour, a good woman offered us a chair and invited us to rest until the rain stopped. Then, excusing herself, she started to pluck a chicken for an officer's supper. Barely seated, as though pushed by an invisible hand, I got up and went out. Mr. Stopford, a little surprised at this sudden movement, followed me. No sooner were we in the middle of the street, than a gust of wind caused the charred walls of Les Halles to collapse, burying under its ruins the woman who had come to talk to us. With the help of two or three men, we began shoveling and after half an hour of work we were able to remove the victim. She was taken to Dehaene's house, opposite the convent, where the parish priest gave her Extreme Unction and where Sister Livine, on Dr. Manning's assurance that she was dead, buried her.

Fortunately the storm did not last long, because many similar accidents would ensue. From 11 o'clock to half past 1, intense bombardment resumed.

2 MARCH – At St. Jean, during the night, the shells killed seventeen soldiers and injured several; civilians also have been hit and three Quaker ambulance cars had much to do this night. – During the day, the shells continued to arrive. Mr. Stopford and I saw shrapnel fall at our feet when we were analyzing the water in the Donck brasserie. The detonation was tremendous and I do not know how the strong blast did not throw us into the open tank beside which we were standing. Ah! If we did not have our good guardian angels. – A Taube is flying over the city.

3 MARCH – Mr. Chopard and the parish priest want to submit the project of the orphanage to Mr. Ligy, president of the Red Cross and then to Mr. Stoffel, chairman of the improvised Committee. All agree, and Mr. Baus, treasurer of the Red Cross, made a donation of 3,000 fr. for the new work.

In the afternoon, the Count and the Countess d'Ursel came to talk to the parish priest about the work of providing bedding and clothing for typhoid patients and refugees. We had to receive them in our living-room-kitchen. That same day, I accompanied the Countess to the fabric shop for material for bedding and shirts; all amounting to over 1,200 fr. The work will be entrusted to two young girl refugees. A list of the poor discovered by the 'Search Party' is given to the generous benefactress. Sister Anna's classroom was disinfected and the doors and windows patched as well as possible.

Christine Bartier will make the bedding there. The large parlor will serve as a depot. With 150 fr. they gave me, I will pay the first workers, pending the 1.500 francs promised by Mr. Young.

When the Friends Ambulance Unit helped create the civilian hospital, Château Elisabeth in Poperinghe, in January 1915, it established a close working relationship with the Countesses van den Steen de Jehay, Directrice of the St. Camille School for Nurses, Brussels, and Countess Louise d'Ursel, Lady in Waiting to H. M. the Queen of the Belgians. The countesses and the FAU had been working towards the same goal – providing aid to the thousands of civilians whose plight was being largely ignored by the various armies around them. Eventually, in April 1915, in order to avoid the overlapping of aid work and thus to increase efficiency, the countesses and the FAU decided to join forces, in an enterprise which would be known as the *Aide Civile Belge (ACB)*. The queen of Belgium became patron. The collaborative enterprise would allow its members to administer civilian aid over a much larger area than they had been able to contemplate individually, beginning with Ypres and Poperinghe, and extending to include the whole of Flanders, together with a large section of the *Departement du Nord* in France, into which large numbers of Belgian refugees had fled. The ACB encouraged the formation of local committees to undertake the distribution of food and clothing and to discuss other needs. The ACB, states Geoffrey Young, was 'an organization which set to work to save all that could be saved of the babies, the families, the education, the feeding the clothing and even the home-industries and lace-making' in the region of Flanders.[33]

4 MARCH – Commander Young has returned to Ypres and Mr. Baker will return to England. The latter has done so much good work in a few days, by devoting himself to all, both civilian and soldiers. May God reward him!

In the morning we prepared Sister Gertrude's classroom, which will be transformed into a workroom. The broken windows were fastened up somehow; there are four sewing machines, a table and some chairs for furnishing. We must begin by altering a few shirts and camisoles. Irma Alleman will lead the work, as I often have to be away, either to do dressings or to accompany Dr. Thompson on his visits to the sick. – Here are the names of the girls of the new class:

Irma Alleman, Jeanne Douflou, Marie Torreborre, Marie Alleman, Anna Desramault, Marie Desramault, Marie d'Haene, Yvonne d'Haene, Gabrielle Sanctorum, Germaine d'Haene.

These workers have made hundreds of clothes for refugees. Germaine Boussaert and Jeanne d'Haene were engaged for bedding; they have already completed over sixty bags of chopped straw for those poor with contagious diseases, whose bedding was burned. – The other girls, too far from the classroom, or frightened by the bombing, work at home. Sometimes, meeting is impossible, and all have to work at home.

Today, around 11 o'clock, the cannonade began again. Several shells (52) fell within our district: near the casements, in Goemare's stable; the Rosseel house collapsed. In the rue des Boudeurs, twenty holes were made in an hour. In the afternoon, in the direction of the Kruisstraat and the *Café Français*. The director, Mr. Herman, returned from Poperinghe to visit us. He was not too pleased with the noisy reception that the cannons gave him and soon returned to Poperinghe.

5 MARCH – Thirty-six shrapnel from noon to half past 3, over the city. A man killed in Château d'Eau. Shells landed on the Dickebusch road and on the Welfare School. The 'Search Party' was in the bombed area. Mr. G. Thompson and Sister Lucia were in rue Vlamertinghe. Doctor Manning and Mr. Littleboy were near the *Café Français*. Mr. Robert Stopford and I were going along the Dickebusch road to visit three farms there. In the fields of the first one, there is an English battery, which was thundering loud enough to tear the eardrums. 'It is no good here,' I said to my companion. 'Let's go to the second farm,' he replied. 'Good!' Hardly had we taken steps in that direction, when . . . bang! . . . bang! . . . bang! Again a battery gave its best! . . . 'Oh', I said, 'we are worse here because the Germans will respond in both directions and we are in the middle!' I had not finished speaking when a shell fell into the field where we were. We took shelter behind a tree. A piece of hot iron came rolling at my feet. I kept it as a souvenir. In our field, there were trenches of a battery. 'Let's hide here,' said Mr. Stopford, 'until the storm has calmed.' For him, with his big rubber boots that would protect him from the water that was there, it was fine; but it was impossible for me to follow him. Boom! Another shell, I hid behind a tree . . . a third shell! . . . Just as Mr. Stopford straightened up, he got a few small pieces of shrapnel in the neck. Fortunately, it was not serious. 'It's nothing,' he said, 'it's a little hot, that's all!' – In the distance, we saw Mr. G. Thompson, who called us. With great difficulty, we managed to free ourselves from the marshes. Seeing us dirty, wet and muddy, one would have thought that we had spent five days in the trenches. The ambulance car arrived to collect us. At the moment it arrived . . . boom! A fourth

shell, followed by a fifth! Mr. Littleboy had no time to turn the car and backed down to *Café Français*. For the fifth time this week, we escaped almost certain death. What a reason to thank God! The Search Party is finished in Ypres. More than 5,000 families have been visited in granaries, attics, apartments, cellars and casements! And all this, most of the time, in full bombardment. But cases of typhoid fever diminish by the day, fortunately. Sister Lucia will accompany the Quakers to Poperinghe, to continue the search, there. I have to stay in Ypres, to help with the work for civilians who remain here. Around half past 5, we returned home: shrapnel welcomed us. This same evening I distributed sixty-six vouchers to poor families of St. Pierre. With this, they can come to the convent tomorrow, around 2 o'clock, to look for clothes.

6 MARCH – Stormy night, but no shells on the city. Around 8 o'clock, the Countess d'Ursel arrived, accompanied by Miss van Hemelryck. She brought us an ambulance car full of clothes, in addition to those that our girls had made. The morning was spent in preparing packages for our poor and our refugees. The Countess and her companion had lunch with us, because we had to save time. At around 2 o'clock, the distribution began; the whole corridor was full. Fortunately, the bombing stopped. Around half past 4, distribution was made; in a few days we will begin again. More than 700 shirts were given out, besides everything else! Around 5 o'clock, the Countess got ready to go, very tired. She asked me to take charge of the new distributions and keep a record of what has been given and to whom. – Dr. Thompson collected me to visit some suspected patients. We found three typhoid cases, who were allowed to be taken to hospital. Among them are two of the Breyne children, refugees from Werwick, which means that eight patients of this family are now in the Sacré Coeur Hospital. Dr. Thompson gave some money to the poor father to buy milk for the two small children that were still with him at home.

7 MARCH – Fairly quiet night. Two dead, rue de Pilkem. After Mass, visit to Saint Jean, Wieltje, Bryke, Kalfvaart. We found two typhoid cases and I had to preach quite hard for the parents of one to let them take him. There have already been twelve cases of typhoid in rue de la Plume.

8 MARCH – Nothing special tonight. After Mass, I made sure that our girls had work to do; then I had to go and talk to some families who wished to go to France. The elderly, children and infirm were

to be driven by the Quakers to the first hostel in Vlamertinghe. Around 11 o'clock, everyone was waiting at the rendezvous, in our dining hall. After Sister Berchmans had given everyone a cup of hot soup, the departure commenced. I accompanied the children in the car, because on reaching their destination, they were to be handed over to their parents who, for the most part, would make the journey on foot. We arrived in Vlamertinghe. Here the picture gets interesting! The children were shaking with cold, and snow was falling in big flakes. One cried! Another lost his belongings; yet another had a package that had come undone! A fourth, stumbling, finally fell into the mud. We had a ten minute walk to the station. On the right arm, I carried a baby; by the left arm, I dragged an old man of 86; on my apron hung one of the two smallest children, another on my rosary and one on my rope. About thirty young children marched in front of us. Picture that procession.

And with all this, the road was crowded with cars and soldiers. From time to time one of the children tumbled . . . and music followed, of course! Fortunately, the brave soldiers helped us as best they could. Finally, after an hour and a half of walking, we arrived at the station. The Quakers' mobile kitchen served the fugitives with good hot soup, bread, meat, cheese and an orange. The stationmaster carefully examined the list I presented to him, which contained the name of each family with the number of its members. One tried to make sure that a family was housed together in the same compartment. – In a few moments the train would leave, but everyone still had a question or a recommendation to make . . . 'Sister, would you pray for me?' 'Sister, my daughter who is still in hospital, will she be able to reach us when she is cured?' 'Sister, my 17 year-old son must stay in Ypres to take care of family affairs; could you keep an eye on him?' 'Sister, where are we going, then?' 'Sister, will it be long before we set off?' . . . They are harrowing scenes, heartbreaking scenes. Poor people! . . . A whistle and the train goes! Off they go . . . Where? . . . I do not know! . . . And for three weeks, from day to day, the same spectacle recurs. – It was one o'clock and the car drove me to the convent to have my meal. Around 2 o'clock I had to guide the Search Party from Ypres to Vlamertinghe, after tea at the Sacré Coeur Hospital; at half past 4 we visited the typhoid cases that we had left with them. During the day, a US Minister, Mr. Treboyen, wanted to see the parish priest, to talk to him about assistance to the needy. The priest accompanied him among the poorest families, who each received 5 francs.

Although everything was pretty quiet today, a shell killed Henri Lemahieu, who was working on his smallholding.

9 MARCH – Three or four shells fell on the ramparts. For a few days, I have done some shopping at Breyne-Devos, 300 fr. of calico for shirts, then at Peckel for 100 fr. and in Gimponprez-Maillard for 197 fr. So, Miss Matilda Maroy took the soup to the poor and elderly, as I had absolutely no time. Today, however, I found some time to go myself. In the afternoon, I accompanied Dr. Thompson to give anti-typhoid injections. At 'Tivoli', rue Lille, we learned that in Driekoningenhoek two refugees from Hollebeke were suffering from typhus. The injections finished, we went to investigate. In a dirty and unkempt house, almost devoid of furniture, we found some children in a terrible state of poverty and neglect. 'How many of you are there in the family?' I asked the mother. – Father, mother and eight children. 'Show us the cards certifying that you have been injected!' 'Six cards! And the others?' – 'My husband and my eldest son are working for the English; my eldest daughter is there, she has a bad cold and will be vaccinated when the others are better.' We asked to look around the home. For bedding, some infectious straw bags. There was a foul odor coming from the bedroom. I opened the window and told the woman to leave the room to air. We went down into the cellar, after our tour of the house, but nowhere could we find the two typhoid cases. We left empty-handed. – 'We will surprise the woman tonight,' said Mr. Dr. Thompson. Around 8 o'clock, there-fore, he came to fetch me with the ambulance car. Along the way, I advised him to keep a stern face, because with his usual gentleness he would gain nothing. I had noticed, on our first visit, that the woman had been leaning against a wooden wall that, perhaps, hid a door.

It was agreed that as soon as we entered we would hasten to the suspicious place and, if necessary, the disguised door would be opened immediately. This is what Dr. Thompson did, while I noti-fied the woman that we had received orders to take all typhoid cases that, because of the proximity of the trenches, were putting our soldiers at risk. We found the two patients in the suspected place, lying on bags. They had temperatures of 40° and 41°, and the son was delirious. Mr. Thompson rebuked the woman in English and did so well that she was fear-stricken. I calmed her and we took them, to their great satisfaction, together with the girl who was less seriously ill. *En route*, we could not help but admire the beautiful spectacle of the rockets that lit up the sky above the city. Too bad that it was for such a sad reason.

10 MARCH – The night is quiet. The parish priest left for Saint-Omer, where he hopes to find a home for orphans. The Dean of the

Holy Sepulchre, the Archpriest of St. Denis and Mr. Duperez, mayor of the city, gave him a warm welcome and he has returned full of hope. During his absence, I made a new purchase of calico for shirts and bedclothes. Over fifty beds and as many blankets were distributed. Around noon, I accompanied the fugitives who wish to search for some security in Vlamertinghe, then, at 2 o'clock, I went with Mr. Thompson to the De Brouwery tavern in Saint Jean where over sixty people presented themselves for the injection against typhus. The evening was spent preparing packages for the poor who wish to leave the city.

11 MARCH – Some shrapnel bombs around noon and one around 3 o'clock. The count of Beaumont du Valee came to have dinner with the parish priest and discuss with him the project of erecting a shelter for orphans. If successful, the parish priest insists that the financial resources for this work are guaranteed and for his part, the Count donated 3000 fr. An American minister who had come to see the Quakers' unit, came, at the same time, to visit our different rooms: that for dressings, that for the injections, the two workrooms for clothing and bedding. He offered to take all the orphaned children with him to America, ensuring that they would want for nothing. But the priest, as both a priest and a father, declined this generous offer. 'These children,' he answered, 'are my children, and I want them to be raised in the Catholic religion. As long as I have enough to feed myself, there will be enough for them. If your charity wants to come to my rescue, I shall be much obliged, but take them away from me, never!' The minister immediately gave him 500 fr. for the makeshift workroom and promised 3,000 fr. for the orphanage.

Several injured in Kruisstraat, although everything is relatively calm.

12 MARCH – The shrapnel bombs were coming thick and fast; but between half past 8 and half past 9, there was an infernal dance. Behind St. Pierre shrapnel was flying everywhere. The Barbry-Baelen child, rue du Canon, was injured. Many poor families from St. Pierre departed for France. In the afternoon, three shells. The door of the 'Patronage' collapsed as did those of the two adjoining houses. – Mr. E. Declercq, a teacher at the College, has found a place for our orphans, with the Trappists in West-Vleteren. Some families to which I have delivered vouchers can come tomorrow to seek a parcel of goods before leaving town. What goodness from the Friends' Ambulance Unit! We can never thank them enough for what they are doing for our poor people of Ypres.

This evening, some time after we had gone back to our beds in the basement, a dozen shells arrived, causing further damage. The front of the Room house collapsed; the office of Mr. D'Huyvettere, the notary and the home of Mr. Craevens, near the Diamanterie, are damaged. Valere Boudry has a broken leg. Mrs. Guwez (mother of Camille) is mortally wounded! It's strange, the shells do not come from the side from which they do usually, but from Langhemarck. I think it was a Zeppelin that passed; between 10 o'clock and 11 o'clock, I heard an unusual noise.

13 MARCH – All those who had received a voucher have taken advantage of the calm to come and get their package. Around noon a 'black bird' flew over the city and dropped three bombs: one at the Lille Gate, one on 'Nazareth' and one on the Sacré Coeur. The Claeys-Coffyn family, that I visited with Mr. Thompson in our tour of the typhoid cases, absolutely refuses to let patients found there be taken to hospital. Three members of the family have already died, others will follow, because we cannot provide them with the necessary care.

14 MARCH – The gentlemen of the Quaker Ambulance collected beds and everything else that might be useful, for the orphanage. We went to the college where two Sisters are lodging in the cellar; they told us what we could take: tables, benches, tanks, etc. The Sisters will accompany the car to West-Vleteren. The weather is superb: a real spring day. During the High Mass, two shells fell in the moat around the ramparts. Good! They should all fall there! The children continued their games and made a new one by imitating the whistle of shrapnel. They abandoned it, shouting and crying, while looking for a shelter, when an explosion was heard. Then everything became dull and silent for a time. – Tonight it is the French cannons that are thundering. These are a succession of lightning flashes without interruption, projecting a blood red glow!

15 MARCH – In the morning, around the station and the Kruisstraat, shells came and destroyed some houses, especially near the gas plant and the 'Kafferwyk'. Dressings with Dr. Manning, where I also act as interpreter for consultations, and distribution of soup cards, occupied the morning. Around 2 o'clock, we had to inform people that all orphans below the age of two should be brought to the convent for 11 o'clock. The parish priest gave me my share of 21 addresses. The parish priest of Saint-Jacques would care for those in Verloren Hoek, and our priest would take care of others. Whilst passing rue de la Gare, to go to the (Kruisstraat) Pannestraat,

good people tried to dissuade me, assuring me that I was risking certain death. Well, that was frank! And at that moment, a shell falling behind the station sent me a burning piece of shrapnel that tore my brown scapular, at chest height. 'Souvenir!' So I went to the Kruisstraat and from there I returned to the commercial area, where I went to warn the refugees from Zonnebeke, in N° 28, that they had to send us the orphans who were with them. On the corner of the street, where I was also searching for two little ones whose mother had been killed a few days ago, the father promised to go himself to Pannestraat, once the storm ceased. A sentry demanded my papers, then with the traditional, 'All right,' allowed me to pass. A few metres away, three shells on Kafferwyk killed Woussen, Braem and the good Sister Biebouw, with a young child. The baby's legs were thrown some distance. Mr. Lepercke picked one up, still with the little foot and shoe on, and took it home. Two other children had legs severed. The ambulance that I sent for arrived immediately and the victims were taken to hospital, after which I returned to the Commercial Area. My parents live in this area, and I found their house open. I went in . . . no-one! Where could my sister be? The cellar was a foot deep in water. On leaving, I saw Emile Devos who assured me that my sister was in the house next door. I did, indeed, find her there and gave her the key to the door, then, while leaving, I said to Devos: 'You, too, would be better off in the cellar, because it's hot here.' 'Oh,' was his answer! 'I am not afraid!' Near the railway barrier, I met my brother and ordered him to join my sister until the horrible bombing had passed. I had hardly taken a few steps when a shell fell in front of the tavern 'Congo' killing Emile Devos and three of the six soldiers who were there looking for victims who were buried under the rubble of the house belonging to the director of the gasworks. This afternoon, three more soldiers and several civilians were wounded. Of the twenty or so people who were there, my brother was the only one left standing. A British soldier rolled at his feet; another, wounded in his side, himself took from his chest a 1lb. piece of shrapnel, saying, 'Souvenir . . . Help please!' My brother, Arsène, supported him and led him to an aid station in rue de la Station, but the poor soldier died on the way. While other wounded made gestures to implore for help, my sister Gabrielle rushed to our aid and took one to the town; another crawled on hands and knees to the neighbouring house. Meanwhile, the ambulance had returned, and all could be taken to hospital. There were, in total, eight dead and twelve wounded; some others had also received minor injuries. On returning to the convent I found my sister and my brother, who wept with fear and emotion. This day was the most awful for the 'Kruisstraat'.

16 MARCH – Relatively quiet night. After patching up some windows and preparing bandages, I had to go with Dr. Thompson to seek new recruits for the typhoid hospital. At noon, upon returning, I found all our dear little orphans gathered in our dining hall, feasting on rice pudding! Poor children, mostly unaware of their misfortune. Sister Marie has arranged the meal; Sister Marie Berchmans examined whether all were well dressed and gave them what they lacked. At around 2 o'clock, the Rev. Mr. Declercq, who will be their director, took them to West-Vleteren; where the Sisters of Gits would welcome them. Large packages of clothes accompany them. This work involving the orphans tires our good priest, but he spares himself little and already he has made it his duty to care for the girls. May God reward him.

A shell around 8.30, near the swimming school and another at 11 o'clock.

17 MARCH – The cannons are thundering and trying to reach a captive balloon. Four shrapnel already before 5 o'clock; half a dozen around 6 o'clock.

The parish priest, together with Commandant G. Young, left for Saint-Omer, where Madame Pannier Ambricourt offers her patronage and has made her home in Wizernes available to the little orphans. Mr. Mayor Duperez agreed to accept the former Benedictine convent in Wisques. Madame Pannier Ambricourt is going to get everything ready for Monday. Four sisters of the Paulines, of Saint-Julien, will take care of the little ones. The Search Party is finished around Ypres. What gratitude we owe to the Friends' Ambulance Unit. The cases of typhus are virtually zero here. Next week, Vlamertinghe and Poperinghe will be explored, as well as their surroundings. With this, the distribution of aid in clothing, bedding, etc., is not slowing down.

19 MARCH – Feast of St. Joseph, patron of our dear Belgium! This reminds me of a strange thing, that is, that almost all the statues of the good saint have had their head removed; one at the parish priest's, at the Reverend Fathers, five in our convent. Is it, perhaps, because, not knowing what to do in our Belgium, St. Joseph has lost his head? No! No! When the time comes, this great protector will show God the trials of his beloved people, suffering for what is right and for justice! And the Lord will give back to him that which has been so unjustly taken away. As for the statues of the Virgin, it is striking to see them miraculously preserved. I refer here to a statue of Mary that was at the entrance of the convent, rue de Lille. On

arrival of the first shell on the house, everything around the statue was in pieces. Only she remained intact; she had just turned her back, a little, to the Lille Gate (to the Germans!) and faced *les Halles*. Soldiers going to the trenches could not but admire this spectacle. Long after our departure from Ypres, after fifty or so shells and shrapnel were thrown at the convent, the little Virgin still remained standing there. The day before I left for England, I returned to Ypres; she was gone. The great statue at the court had made the same move, turning its back to the Germans. Many of these images made a deep impression on the soldiers.

A new case of typhus, Menin road. It is an 18 year-old girl, who had refused inoculation. After lengthy negotiations, the mother agreed to let her leave. At the moment that we were placing her in the ambulance, the Germans began bombing the area; lead bullets rained down around us. The canvas of the cover was torn in three places. The patient cried and we hurried to leave Smisje. No one was injured, only the windows suffered. Up to Bascule, shells were constantly bursting behind us. It seemed that we were being pursued!

20 MARCH – An aerial struggle began: there were nine aeroplanes, including five Germans and four Allies. The Germans were forced to withdraw. Miss Hallaert was slightly wounded in the head by a lead bullet. Two, three shrapnel bombs, followed by a shell that knocked down four houses in Kruisstraat, then it was our cannons that occasionally startled residents. – This afternoon, from the rue Menin, where we were at about 3 o'clock, we saw flames rising from the Donck farm between Saint-Julien and Langhermarck. The farmer had typhus and had to be visited that day. We found three hundred French soldiers and thirty refugees in the courtyard. After leaving the patient in a safe place, we returned to the farm. The fire had been caused by the carelessness of some soldiers who had made a fire in a store-room covered with straw. Everyone was working to extinguish the fire or to rescue furniture and effects. We returned to our patient. The woman to whom we had entrusted him asked us to visit her sick daughter. She was suffering from typhus and had a fever of 40.5°. Dr. Thompson found her too ill to move and left the operation until the next day.

21 MARCH – Aeroplane chase from early morning! Shrapnel killed a man in the Sacré Coeur and two women in the Kruisstraat. – Then fifty shells! The parish priest received bad news: the mayor of Saint-Omer told him that the orphanage has to be given over to

the soldiers. Yet he did not lose confidence: Providence is here! Our girls do good work, but they dared not come to find work today; the shelling was too violent. I took it to them myself.

22 MARCH – Great noise of rifles and machine guns. When will it end? The workers came to work. Visits with Dr. Thompson to the typhoid cases. Many injections in the afternoon. Customers for the physician and the dressings are numerous. The soldiers (250) at rest here for five days, are preparing the room reserved for them. Our workers sing whilst working. What a pity that we should at all times be expecting a bomb to come and turn everything upside down.

Someone came to warn me not to leave the convent, as the Minister of Broqueville was to honor us with a visit. The parish priest, who was at home, was also warned. The Minister arrived, accompanied by the Count de Lichtervelde, Commander Lannoy, the hero of Liège, and Commandant G. W. Young. I made him visit our dining hall, where Dr. Wallice was giving injections to forty people; the sewing room, where Dr. Manning, assisted by Miss Cloostermans, was bestowing his care upon the wounded; the classroom, where two girls were busy with bedding, and that in which there were a dozen others making clothes. Finally, the room that served as a store containing medicines, canned food, condensed milk, etc., for refugees and babies, etc.

He also saw the work of our brave English soldiers, and could not express enough appreciation and astonishment at the sight of so many diverse improvised works in bombed buildings and amid a heap of ruins! He thanked the Friends Unit for all the well-organized work, he also thanked our valiant and heroic priest, whose highly courageous dedication he admired, then he offered me his hand, also expressing his warm thanks, and ensuring us of his assistance and protection at all times.

23 MARCH – Nothing except loud cannon fire, from time to time. Clothing distribution; injections with us and in home visits.

24 MARCH – Some typhoid cases are transported, the sick visited; we got to St. Julien, through a dam and a meadow smashed up by shells.

25 MARCH – The night was disturbed only between half past 3 and 5 o'clock, when fifty shrapnel bombs arrived.

More than 65 girls, prepared by Sister Antoinette, Sister Jeanne and Marie Vanuxem, came to fulfill their Easter duty in the chapel of the Soeurs Noires.

While going with Dr. Thompson to visit refugees, on the Zonnebeke road, we found a case of diphtheria at N°. 45, a typhoid at N°. 21 and two cases of scarlet fever at N°. 33. All were taken to the hospital just after lunch.

A dozen shells, destroying two houses, killing two soldiers and wounding two French girls near the communal house of Vlamertinghe lead us to assume that the Germans are approaching a little.

26 MARCH – A young refugee from Zonnebeke was killed by a shell, in the afternoon. – More than 200 Scottish soldiers have settled into our nursery school.

The Reverend Declercq left for Wisques with six orphans from Watou and four Sisters of St. Julian who had been staying, after the outbreak of war, with the Sisters of the same Order in St. Jean ter Biezen. – The 'Search Party' began its searches at Vlamertinghe. On the main road from this village to Ypres, we found twelve typhoid cases that were taken to the Elisabeth Hospital, established and run by the Quakers of the Friends Unit, like that of the Sacré Coeur, and where the Countess d'Ursel and Countess Van der Steen Jehay are working with admirable dedication.

27 MARCH – During the quiet, two or three Boches came to inspect. – Mr. Stoffel, who is carrying out the office of mayor, has received many crates of clothes for refugees. The distribution was made without delay, to the delight of the poor. I defer, therefore, the sharing of my goods, on the advice of the parish priest, until Mr. Stoffel's treasure is exhausted.

28 MARCH – The British airmen hunted two or three German Taubes, that had dropped a bomb behind the station. Some soldiers were there with horses; they are unhurt. – Commandant Young gave me a list made by the vicar Mr. Van Walleghem, which will serve as guide to arrange two large bundles of clothes for the poor of Clytte.

29 MARCH – Around half past 7, shrapnel bombs on the dock. A soldier who was in Mr. Vergracht's store had a leg blown off. Several horses were killed. An aeroplane chase! Bombardment of Kruisstraat. Some patients along the Ypres – Boesinghe canal were visited.

30 MARCH – Complete calm. The young workers brought me their work. Everything is ready for la Clytte.

77 shirts for men
130 for women
143 for boys
148 for girls
72 for infants

In addition, some trousers, jackets, skirts, camisoles, socks, to be shared between 84 families.

Dr. Thompson took me to continue his visits to typhoid cases of the Saint-Jacques parish, outside the city. Many were found: Vanden Bergh, Hughe's wife, the father of the Ghelein family, etc.

31 MARCH – Around half past 7, dozens of shrapnel bombs on the docks and rue Dixmude. A young man (J. Seghers) and six soldiers were wounded. Today, workmen in the Sœurs Noires found the body of Celine Pladys, killed Nov. 11, 1914, half-eaten by rats.

1 APRIL – TB patients were visited today: a man, street Thourout; Lebbe; Kalfvaart, and the wife of Ch. Van Overschelde who had expired on our arrival.

2 APRIL – Around half past 11, visit from shrapnel bombs, especially towards the rue de Menin where a woman was seriously injured. This afternoon, the Countess d'Ursel brought us four American ladies from *Appui Belge*. They brought us lots of goods and colonial commodities for distribution among children. The curé made me responsible for the inventory, which, I think, must be at 3,000 fr., not including the clothes.

3 APRIL – Noise of cannons and occasionally a shell. Isidore Samyn, a refugee from Werwicq, native of Moorslede, badly injured. – The boxes and packages gave me a fine task! When unpacking I found a package marked 'Miss Hoyt'. It is for an injured girl who is at the Sacré Coeur. Towards evening, I took it to her and I took the opportunity of visiting the typhoid wards. Nobody had wanted me to send them there! All have praise for the good care they are given by the English doctors and Sisters. Three girls are dying. The reverend vicar Callens is at their bedside.[34]

4 APRIL – The Germans have taken a British trench tonight. The evening brings us twenty shells. One fell on *les Halles*, where we had hidden the chandeliers from St. Martin's Church. All are broken or damaged. The Belle hospice, the Baus home, the Vanheule home, rue

Longue-du-Marais, and that of the Room family, rue St. Elizabeth, have also had one. Mr. Room and Mr. Vanhove were killed, and in the adjoining house, the husband and wife Dethoor-Deweerdt have injuries. Their two children, Henry and Blanche, seriously wounded, died a few hours later at the Sacré Coeur. At the orphanage St. Elizabeth, where there is an English ambulance, two soldiers killed and six wounded.

The Countess d'Ursel has sent me the men's clothes she had promised. Twelve little old women left for Pontoise and fifteen old men for Corbeil (France). Sister Livine and sister Lucia accompanied them. There are parties all over the place!

6 APRIL – Commander Young came to take the parish priest to La Panne, where the Governor has summoned them. – Visiting the sick, we found two new cases of typhus. – Around half past 6, a new bombardment of the city. In the Old Clothes Market, several people were killed under the rubble of a house. Two old women were injured, one in the arm, another in the head. I dressed their wounds and advised them to go to rue Thourout and wait in the casements until the end of the bombing. They can then stay in the cellars of the Gillebert brewery, where we can look after them properly, then, at the first opportunity, they will be taken to France.

7 APRIL – Another sad day for us! While Fr. Versteele went to collect three orphans between Saint-Julien and Langhermarck, I went to my side with the driver D. Roose, to collect: three in Potyse, four in Hemelrykje, four in Saint Jean. I had just returned to give some refreshment to our little colony, before dispatching it off to Wisques-lez-Saint-Omer, when they began to bombard our convent. Over 250 Scottish soldiers were there. Seeing the danger, I took the smallest of my dear charges and made them all get into a motor car for the Sacré Coeur, where they could dine more comfortably. *En route* I warned commander Young of the danger that threatened the soldiers and the wounded who were waiting at the convent to have their dressings done.

Mr. Fox and commander Young went immediately to the convent, where I joined them after handing my little ones into the care of the hospital Sisters. Three shells hit their target, killing four soldiers on the spot; three others died within a fortnight. One of the cooks who was busy cutting the meat was so overcome that, after throwing his knife away, he ran amok in the cellars of the Sœurs Noires, where he then collapsed, only regaining consciousness an hour later. While crossing the street, Sister Martha, who was running away from the

Sœurs Noires' convent, saw the sentinel fall inert at her feet. A girl of twenty, half-scared, hid behind one of the soldiers, who rolled at her feet, mortally wounded, while she remained unharmed. Monsieur Roose, the vicar, who was celebrating Mass for the repose of the souls of Room and Van Hove, in the Soeurs Noires, was making the offering when the bombing began. There was general panic, everyone fled; two or three women fainted. The priest continued the Mass alone, in a low voice, the choir also having sought refuge in cellars. One of the fugitives who had taken shelter in the tavern Het Truweeltje, rue des Chiens, was buried under the rubble. The parish priest found him, got him out, and had him carried to the Sacré Cœur, where he died that morning. Two soldiers, who were preparing lunch for the officers, were killed in Mr. Vermeulen's brewery. Vermeulen had a slight head injury; I dressed it immediately.

In Bukkerstraat, a shell fell on the Castelein bakery killing the worker Adelin Houtekeit and wounding Philipaert. Mrs. Castelein sustained twenty-three injuries, including several that were fatal, and she was taken to the Sacré Coeur, where she died the next day. All these events succeeded one another within an hour. These are moments that one must have lived through to be aware of the fear and anxiety they spread. – The parish priest, always courageous, and though exhausted with fatigue, went to the Soeurs Noires to celebrate Mass and perform the funeral of Henry and Jean Dethoor. – Once the newly-wounded were installed in the hospital, the ambulances drove our orphans to Wisques.

8 APRIL – The bombing continues. Some old men went to Pontoise and some old women to Corbeil. In the rue des Trèfles, a poor woman suffering from typhus was taken to the Sacré Coeur, leaving three small children in the care of the unfortunate husband; the youngest was sick and was only five months old. Immediately, the parish priest took charge. For 20 fr. a month, a refugee will look after the child.

9 APRIL – Many wounded are now seeking advice or dressings with Dr. Manning. Around noon, I arrived at the convent with a baby, I had found her in her crib, alone and crying. Poor little thing! A small collection of necessities was gathered for her and she was entrusted to the woman I mentioned yesterday. Austrian shells arrived today, they say. They can be recognised by their strange whistle.

10 and 11 APRIL – We are in Boesinghe. A Taube came to explore. The French, with their '75', shot it down in flames.

12 APRIL – Burial of Mrs. Castelein. – The corridor and the refectory of the convent were full of women and children crying in terror waiting for the ambulances to lead them to safety. It was Sister Marie Berchman's task to calm them and serve them soup, sandwiches and a piece of chocolate. Each mother received one or two cans of condensed milk. Around 11 o'clock, the ambulances were there. The men took the lead, on foot. Everyone will meet at the station in Vlamertinghe.

13 APRIL – The Taubes returned yesterday afternoon. Mr. Herman, our Reverend Director, came to pay us a visit – a visit that he did not dare to prolong, as a few cannon shots could only be the prelude to a new bombardment. Around 9 o'clock, the cannon blasted violently. They say that they are ours that are hunting aeroplanes.

15 APRIL – Yesterday, our good priest took the Blessed Sacrament to eighteen sick or injured, who are exempt from their Easter duty. It was touching to see him pass in rochet and velum[35], preceded by two altar boys carrying the bell and the torch. But yet again faith shows us the moving spectacle of an infinite God, visiting his poor creatures in their humblest recesses to reward their love. – Many soldiers arrived yesterday evening. – German forces sent shells along the canal, close to the Kruisstraat, where the remains of the city lie. Did they think they were fortifications? This morning Michel Ossieur, in handling an unexploded shell, made it explode. He had his legs blown off and died a few moments later. Around half past 10, when visiting the typhoid cases, Dr. Thompson and I could see a German plane that was launching bombs on British soldiers. We had to park and more than one bomb fell close to us. We were caught up in the game! Five new cases of typhus. Two others between Saint-Julien and Langhemark. We are cited by a French chaplain.

17 APRIL – Yesterday, a German airplane was shot down between Vlamertinghe, Dickebusch and Poperinghe. Another large section of wall collapsed in our convent. A Boche plane was shot down near the Dixmude Gate. One of the airmen was dead; the other seriously injured. There are a lot of planes, because of the good weather. Whilst going to visit the two typhoid cases we had been told about yesterday, Dr. Fox, Dr. X . . . and I were obliged to get out of the car to climb over the wire that stretched for a kilometre around the

Hoflack farm. A French corporal asked for our papers. Only Dr. Fox was able to present any, and as they were English, we could not pass. Fortunately, after about ten minutes of waiting, I saw the chaplain who had asked us to go in search of the sick and the barrier was lifted immediately. The farm had been burned down two days earlier by the Germans and we found the sick in the barn. There were three and they were taken to the Sacré Coeur.

4 o'clock – Minute by minute, the cannon gave a tremendous blow. An aeroplane dropped three bombs!

7 o'clock – A violent attack began and triple artillery were in full swing.

18 APRIL – The record for cannon fire is today! No less than thirty per minute! And that since 7 o'clock in the morning until 1 o'clock. The gunners seemed to relax a little! It was about time! The deafening sound would eventually make us lose our heads! The Allies took five trenches near Gheluvelt and took five prisoners. But what ruins! On the Elverdinghe road, where we went in search of two typhoid cases, it is nothing but a pile of stone, brick, glass. Opposite the church, the car had to stop and the journey had to be continued on foot. Not a living soul! Everywhere was deserted. – A large, half-demolished waggon loaded with furniture seemed to be waiting for the moment to leave. A shell fell behind us, sending us some pieces of wood, earth and glass. It came to shake us out of our consternation, and two officers, emerging from I know not where, took advantage of this moment to take my photograph in the middle of the dust cloud in which I found myself. A second shell hit the church at the time Mr. Armstrong was preparing to set the car in motion, to go home, and while the crashing glass and clatter of stones continued, a large piece of iron came tearing down between Armstrong and myself and broke eleven pipes of our car, from where water began to escape immediately. No way to drive after that.

Four Canadian officers *en route* to Elverdinghe, hastily turned around and Dr. Fox begged them to take me to the Sacré Coeur, where Mr. G. W. Young hastened to send an ambulance to the rescue of the damaged vehicle.

19 APRIL – The attack did not end until about 10 o'clock in the evening. This morning, after the service for Mr. Dethoor, while taking the body to the cemetery, the arrival of a shrapnel bomb forced the procession to retrace its steps. In Bascule, where I was at about 9 o'clock with Dr. Fox, all the inhabitants had fled into the

fields. At the cemetery, crosses, portraits, etc., were blown to pieces as far as Cattotjes. In a house that had collapsed, we found two dead and one injured. The corpse of a young girl, struck in her flight, had been picked up by Mr. Vanderghote, the engineer. I recognized her to be the cousin of Julia Lenoir, one of my students; she must be 22 years old. Our tour of the sick was quite interrupted, that day. It was the first day of the second major bombing, which would last a fortnight. Near the Goemaere Gate, children were still playing in the street and the birds were still singing, but after the first shell the song fell silent, our feathered friends flew to safer places and all the urchins, crying and trembling, ran into the casements to tell their parents about it. Having arrived at the home of Jules De Kin, we were unable to leave the house and we took refuge under the stairs. During the twenty minutes we were there, more than sixty shells succeeded each other, a dozen did not explode; two fell in front of where we were, on the new sacristy. Three times, Dr. Fox wanted to go and have a look, but each time the arrival of a new shell forced him to close the door. The last burst in front of the house and the shrapnel, as big as a fist, came rolling at our feet. The doctor picked it up, piping hot, in his handkerchief to keep as a souvenir. Finally, after half an hour spent between life and death, a relative lull enabled us to take a breath and to go out. We found lots of horses killed or wounded. A soldier, who left his shelter at that moment, was ordered by Dr. Fox to finish off the severely injured horses. While the doctor continued his search, I returned to the convent where, undoubtedly, wounded were waiting for me. I found, in fact, little J. Demeester, Passchendaele, 11 years old, struggling against death. He had his right arm and left leg blown off. Mr. Roose gave him absolution and an hour later he took his last breath. His mother and two other children were killed in the blast, and his little sister, 5 years old, was mortally wounded. The poor father is in the hospital, among the typhoid cases. Joseph Hoff, already previously injured and healed, was killed. That same day, in the afternoon, Victorine Vanux, Mrs. Lacante and her sons, two of the Devos children and two officers, sustained serious injuries. From a collapsed house, that buried three people, a woman managed to emerge unscathed. Mr. Alph. Van den Driessche was beheaded, his wife and son are under the rubble. Two other dead were brought to the convent; there are two more in Bolle, rue Carton, and eleven among the soldiers of the 81st French division's ambulance unit, which has, withal, over forty injured. This is the price of five reconquered trenches, no doubt. In short, a terrible day.

20 APRIL – The terrible bombing of yesterday brings new beginnings: Sister Vincentina, Sister Jeanne and the Sisters of St. Joseph's school left for Poperinghe. Today, the victims are numerous, again. In the afternoon, a shell fell on the Donck brewery, Menin Gate, killing twenty-three people of the fifty who had taken refuge there. On my way there, I met a little girl of 9 years of age, Jeanne Meersdom, dragging her little brother of 7 and her sister of 5, fleeing Poperinghe! Here is the sad story that she told me: 'Oh! Sister, we have to go to Poperinghe. It's Yvonne who told me (Yvonne, her sister, aged 14); she has had her arm severed, and she said she was going to die and that I have to take care of my brother and my little sister since I am the oldest, now, and mummy died of typhus a few days ago.' 'And daddy?' I asked. 'Oh, Sister! Daddy must be dead too, as he was speaking to Mr. Versavel when a shell came and exploded near the bed, at the feet of Mr. Versavel. For a moment, Daddy was surrounded by stars and then everything was dark because all the lights were off. All this happened so quickly. We had just finished our prayers and we were playing in a corner of the cellar. We were saved by climbing over the dead and wounded. That's why you see us all dirty and full of blood!' This poor child had a broken arm and the two youngest had serious injuries on their legs, from which blood was dripping. I took the poor little ones with me and Claeys, whom I met, loaded the boy onto his back and took the little girl in his arms. Meanwhile, the ambulance had arrived; the children were bandaged and taken to the casements behind the Saint-Jacques church (military bakery); all the wounded, helped by Miss Cloostermans, had managed to creep out of the cellars and were taken to the Sacré Coeur where, in this sad circumstance, the English doctors, once again, showed their admirable dedication. The night was spent relieving injured, several had arms and legs blown off.

22 APRIL – What sad surprises are still awaiting us! Yesterday, on returning from our visits to the sick, around 5 o'clock, French soldiers (Hindus) were fleeing the trenches. We encountered them screaming and shouting that the Germans had poisoned them! Many died on the road; others experiencing asphyxia clamored for a little milk. I returned to the house while the doctor, forced to continue, returned to Bryke where he had to care for a woman. But the latter, frightened by the bombing, had fled into the fields, where Dr. Fox found her, after an hour of searching, with her newborn baby. She was taken immediately to the Sacré Coeur. At the convent, I found still more soldiers, victims of poison gas; they were served hot condensed milk.

This was the first large-scale use of gas in the war. The Germans had released some 6,000 cannisters of chlorine gas along a four-mile stretch of front. It was carried by the air current across no-man's land into the Allied trenches. This horrific and deplorable tactic took everyone by surprise and, without masks or any other means of protection, large numbers of French colonial troops were overcome by the poison. Many were killed instantly; others died later in excruciating agony and countless more were maimed for life. And those who fled in panic from the trenches made easy targets for machine gun fire. The line was held by courageous Canadian troops, until British and French reinforcements arrived to help stem the attack, but there were already enormous numbers of casualties, particularly among the 13th Battalion of the Canadian Expeditionary Force. All available FAU ambulances worked day and night, until all casualties had been cleared – up to 920 being carried in one day. Some civilians occupying farms and other dwellings near the front lines were also caught up in the terrible events, and were killed or injured in the attack.

25 APRIL – 37 new poison cases this morning (on the morning of 23). Impossible to take them further than the civil hospital where they are housed in the cellars. The less sick were caring for the others. That was the same day, I believe, that Canadian soldiers received a shower of asphyxiating shells that have killed many of them. We too have received our share: one on the convent and two or three nearby. It is terrible! Water flowed from my eyes, my lips turned blue, I was almost choking. The sensation was so dreadful that I was almost climbing the walls. I grabbed a bottle of ammonia and sniffed strongly, then I went down to the cellar and sprinkled it with the liquid. After a while I felt better, and began to block up all the windows. 'Oh! These shells are going to force me from here,' I said to myself. Indeed, civilians were being urged to evacuate the city. Joseph Cottonier Eugene Talon, Mr. Six, Schoonheere, Vanden Abeele and Ghekiere volunteered to stay despite the growing danger, to search for the wounded and bury the dead. The priest obtained a residence permit and, unfortunately, they will have no shortage of work!

26 APRIL – During recent days, the residents remaining in the town have been evacuated. Reverend Roose also left to take his mother to Poperinghe, intending to return, but he was not allowed back. The Palace of Justice, the ancient residence of Jansenius, and the only historical monument that was still standing, has been

bombed. The ambulance of the Friends Unit had to go to Poperinghe, but we are not abandoned. Two doctors and three assistants, residents at the St. Augustine Inn, between Ypres and Vlamertinghe, come from time to time to ensure that we do not need their help.

A '420' finished off Saint Joseph's School and the College.[36] There are dead bodies all over, many of which will have to remain there a fortnight. Sometimes it is impossible to recognize whether they are civilians or soldiers. As it is forbidden to civilians to touch the bodies of the dead soldiers, they have to be left there, abandoned on the street or in an empty house.

The church of Saint-Jacques is burning. The tower must have received a shell. A shell fragment was found near the church. The priest rushed there with Sister M. Berchmans, Sister Livine and Jos. Cottenier. The priest climbed the roof of the Providence to stop the fire. The picture of Notre Dame du Rosaire was brought to our convent, and a lot of objects belonging to the priest and to the Providence were saved and put in the house in front of Dr. Tyberghien, rue Street Saint Jacques.

27 APRIL – Tonight, new incendiary shells fell on the church and the house where we had carried the salvaged items! All work yesterday was useless. But these hardships do not stop our dedicated pastor, and no one will ever be able to appreciate the extent of his charitable works, about which many facts remain unknown even to those who are the object of them, and who, fleeing the danger, sought more security elsewhere.

The sick, the wounded, refugees, children, the elderly, prisoners, orphans, infants, all were helped, rescued by his tireless concern. The erection of the orphanages at Wizernes, for boys, and Wisques, for girls, with over 100 children each, represent only a minor parte. – So it is with a feeling of deep satisfaction that we saw H. M. King Albert award him and his friend and collaborator, Commander G. W. Young, the Cross of the Order of Leopold. – Our best congratulations for this distinction so valiantly gained. – How much more beautiful will be the reward that the King of kings is reserving for these generous benefactors.

MAY 1 – On 29 April, we found the intact body of Juliet Liege; she must have been a victim of the Tribunal fire. She still had on her a great number of bonds saved from a burning house. A few feet away lay two corpses that some recognized and, further away, that of an old woman who was unrecognizable. She wore a blue apron; in her pocket there was a wallet containing 5 fr. and some centimes; her lace-making tile, without doubt her only means of income, was at her side.[37]

As there is no hospital in or around the town, Miss Cloostermans prepared a room in the barracks, which also serves as a *gendarmerie*, to treat the wounded. J. Lorrain and, two days later, Claeys, died there after some hours of suffering. Those who still have some hope of life are transported by the Quaker ambulance.

3 MAY, if I am not mistaken. – From time to time, some joyful incident throws a little ray of sunshine on our present miserable existence. After much searching, on the indications of the parish priest, we discovered an old woman in the heart of a bombed and half-collapsed house. She had not eaten for two days and could barely walk. While Miss Cloostermans continued the search, assisted by two gendarmes who accompanied us, I set out to drag the woman over the pile of bricks blocking the passage to the ambulance car. It had been brought to transport our infirm by Miss Fyfe, a Scottish lady who has been devoted to the relief of the wounded since the beginning of the war. A gallant Canadian, seeing my efforts, came out of his hiding place and offered me his help. Hearing the whistling, a second soldier came out: together, they would have easily helped the stalwart old woman; but she would not listen. Beginning to cry, she sank down and shouted indignantly: 'What? Never in my life have I given my arm to a man and now I should give it to a soldier!' He had to yield. I motioned to the soldiers that I would drag her out myself, mainly because I wanted to get the job done quickly, as the bombing was becoming violent. When she got to the car, in rue de Lille, the old woman refused to get in: first, she wanted to buy 3 cents worth of tobacco! I gave her 1 fr., saying she could get as much as she liked in Poperinghe. Finally, she decided to take a place in the car already crowded with dogs, cats and bird cages that Miss Fyfe had found here and there! This lady has returned several times to offer her services; but the great saviours of our Yproise population are and will continue to be, along with our good pastor, the members of the Friends Unit. The latter have extended their generosity as far as making their charitable excursions during the heaviest bombardments, when the greatest numbers were trying to escape. This greatly increased the danger to themselves, despite the speed of their smaller cars, in which they preferred to drive the fugitives nimbly to the rue Vlamertinghe, where large ambulances collected them to drive them up to Poperinghe. These comings and goings were often repeated up to six and seven times with the greatest

danger to their own lives, but for the greater benefit of the inhabitants, who, once the bombing ended or slowed down, often gave up their escape plan, saying that the Germans had probably finished wasting their guns on our poor city. And that is how many became victims, because the Germans began again with a rage!

The Baelden and Baratto families, all refugees, rue Trèfles, have been well tested today. The Baelden and Baratto women were killed instantly. The father Baratto has two fatal injuries, the only son, of 11 years of age, has a cracked skull, Mrs. Baelden's sister, a refugee from Houthulst, has a broken leg. The Baelden father is covered in small wounds from head to toe. His 7 year-old son has had his foot severed below the ankle. The three little ones are safe. All were transported to the convent. – In seeking help for all these unfortunate people, other sad spectacles present themselves to us: here is a man caught between the shafts of a hand cart, laden with packages, with his wife and children; in the distance a man directs affairs, holding a bundle in his hand, while another package is thrown away; then there is a soldier lying under his dead horse. We found no-one in the Sacré Coeur, and Miss Josephine ran to St. Augustine. Dr. Van Robaeys handed over the cases of broken limbs and the Friends took the wounded to Poperinghe, except the Baratto father and son, who succumbed a few hours later. The other three children went to swell the number of orphans gathered in Wisques. The valuables found on the victims were buried for a few days.

Today, 4 May, the ambulance came to take a dozen people with their bundles of tatters. At all cost, it was necessary to lodge three others from rue Thourout. Through the piles of bricks and debris, we came upon three little old women. While they were getting ready, I went to the nearby casements to see whether there were any civilians still inside. There were only soldiers and I engaged two of them to come and help me carry the ladies. As we came through the door, carrying the last, a large shell flattened the house! What a joy to know we were all saved! And what reason to thank God for having protected us from this new danger!

6 MAY – A shell fell on our sewing class, at about 3 o'clock. The stairs next to it collapsed around midday. The parish priest and I were chasing . . . a goat! She had strayed from rue de Lille and we sent her to join two of her companions on the grass at the Soeurs Noires. – A calf found yesterday will be slaughtered today and the meat shared between people who are still in Ypres. The son of Ghekiere, the farmer who was killed a few weeks ago, is also injured.

7 MAY – A 420 mm shell has just demolished a house on the rue de Menin, near the lions. I strongly fear that there will be victims; sometimes I have been shown small bunkers where one believes that one is in perfect safety. However, it was suspected that there was someone there that evening, despite them not being seen by the four gendarmes. Seven soldiers and three or four civilians who were still in the cellars of the Boone brewery are also leaving the city, as well as Mr. Van Robaeys, Mr. Commissioner and Mr. Stoffels. The latter may be cited, like the parish priest and commander Young, and I am surprised that he has not received the award of the Order of Leopold.

The son of the widow, Mrs. Callewaert, has just left town. He has a seriously injured arm. Everyone has gone from Kalfvaart. There must be corpses buried under the rubble, because this neighbour-hood was bombed suddenly and furiously tonight. The parish priest has sent his workers who, with the help of two policemen, have already discovered two corpses. Joseph Cottonier witnessed a sad spectacle in a half-demolished house. They found the kitchen door tied shut with a rope. On the table was the bank-book of Blanche V . . . and in the corner, an old man, overcome and terrified, all his limbs trembling. Joseph brought the gendarmes. At first glance, the poor man thought that they were Germans, but they soon reassured him and convinced him that they had come to rescue him. He found it impossible to walk, because he was so weak; he was carried on a stretcher to the cart, where he had to lie on the two bodies being taken away. Oh! How pleased this unfortunate man was when he saw me! 'Ah,' he said, 'I knew that the Blessed Virgin would come to my rescue!' I asked him who he was; Here is his story: 'I am Leopold Mahieu, refugee from Moorslede, who, a few weeks ago, arrived here in the home of V . . . who, three days ago, left with my wallet containing 16,000 fr., after having tied the door. Since then I have not drunk or eaten. I have not ceased to pray that the Blessed Virgin send someone to help me. If you had not come, I would have starved to death or been hit by a shell. I am 86 years old. My children are in Moorslede. My business is in the hands of the notary of Passchendaele.' After he had taken a drink and made his confession, in accordance with his wishes, he declared again what he had told me, in the presence of the parish priest Delaere, Jos. Cottonier, E. Talon, and two gendarmes. The Quakers have taken him to Poperinghe.

8 MAY – The body of Louise Devos was found. She had a little basket containing some items for sewing, a catechism, her savings and pension booklets. There is no bread for the 35 to 40 people still

in town. The parish priest gave me Jos. Cottonier and Eug. Talon as domestic servants and I became master baker. The bakery of E. Penseel, to which he handed us the key before leaving, was at our disposal. We found six and a half sacks of flour. The oven heated, work began in the middle of a terrible bombing! But soon I had to leave the job, because Mr. G. W. Young came to evacuate the last remaining inhabitants and refugees. My two apprentices continued to divide the dough and form the loaves, while Sister Livine took care of the oven. I went, in baker's costume, in search of the civilians to be taken. In most of the casements, there were only soldiers. However, in that at the Lille Gate there were still fourteen refugees who, with great difficulty, I cleared out. In that of Bukkerstraat I found a wounded soldier, who was taken to a second car that had arrived at that moment. The Quakers left for Poperinghe with their little colony, and I ran back to find my loaves; I arrived just in time to put them in the oven with the help of Jos. Cottonier, because Eug. Talon had gone to see his wife and children who were to leave for Poperinghe, as were the Schoonheere and Six families. Our batch was very successful! We have 74 beautiful loaves!

9 MAY – Everyone has deserted; even the priest's assistants, who were occupied in burying the corpses, were forced to interrupt their work to follow the caravan. Ourselves, we have prepared our bags for any eventuality!

12 o'clock – Mr. G. W. Young arrived with several men and three ambulances. They dined with us, because this is the only hotel in town.

1 o'clock – An officer came by motorcycle, to warn us that it is time to leave the city, because it is feared that the Germans will soon break through; the Allies cannot hold on if reinforcements do not arrive quickly.

Another danger is the deserters who roam the city in a drunken state. We shared our bread between soldiers and gendarmes, as we leave soon.

Half past 7 – A second officer was sent to warn us of the imminent danger: we were being dispatched; we must evacuate before 2 o'clock. There was time only to load our bags while a car went to the Hospice of Saint Jean and the Nazareth in search of Sister Godelieve and Sister Dymphne.

After a long look at our ruins, and especially at the image of the Blessed Virgin, still standing above the front door of our devastated convent, despite the barrage of about thirty shells and shrapnel that were exploding above us, we abandoned, broken-hearted, our beloved home and our good town of Ypres. On the way, we met the reinforcements sent. The road was crowded with Scottish soldiers who had left the trenches.

On arriving in Poperinghe we learned that our dear Reverend Mother and the Sisters had continued their pilgrimage, first to Proven, then to France, but nobody could tell us where they have come to rest. The parish priest will live in the deanery where Sister Marie and Sister Antoinette will also lodge. Sr. Marie Berchmans, Sister Livine and I will be in one of the hospital sheds.

Between 8–10 May, the FAU received orders for the definitive evacuation of Ypres. The curé and the nuns had sworn not to leave until there were no longer any citizens remaining in the town and who might need their help. But there was now nobody left among the blazing ruins. The clerics, together with their assorted bundles, were removed to the relative safety of Poperinghe, together with two lorry-loads of salvaged ecclesiastical items. Geoffrey Young, often accompanied by Curé Delaere, continued to organise the rescue of valuables from the town, including the town archives, and the art and other treasures from the convents and churches. There had been prolific looting and everything that could easily be reached by deserters had already been sacked, but members of religious orders had buried or otherwise concealed anything and everything of great value, before abandoning the town. They sent the curé detailed maps and instructions that would lead to stashes of religious, historic and economic worth. Those goods that were successfully salvaged were removed to a storage warehouse that Curé Delaere had secured in St Omer.

10 MAY – The cool of the night did not prevent us from sleeping, nor did the lack of a bed, which we got used to in the cellar where we had stayed for seven months or so. We will go to Bailleul today to look for Sister Livine's Superior, whom we were told was there. My parents, who are also refugees there, will perhaps be able to give us the necessary indications.

11 MAY – My sister, Gabrielle, accompanied us, yesterday, to the Soeurs Noires in rue d'Ypres where Sister Livine found her fellow sisters. As for me, I continued my journey to Saint-Omer, to *L'Appui Belge* and then to Sister Marguerite of the Soeurs Noires. Here, among the typhoids, I found our Sister Germaine – of whose illness I had been completely unaware. – She is very ill and could not recognize me.

The record card detailing Soeur Germaine's admission to Hospital Elisabeth, Poperinghe, on 1 May shows that she was suffering from typhoid, diagnosed by the presence of B typhosis in the blood. The record card states that she had been evacuated to the typhoid hospital at Malassise the following day, and from there to the convent at St Omer on 12 July. However, either the date given for the latter evacuation is inaccurate, or Soeur Marguerite is mistaken about the date that she saw Soeur Germaine.[38]

Sister Berchmans will also take accommodation in the deanery. I will stay at the hospital where I will busy myself with some sewing for Countess van der Steen. I found my customary bedroom, that is to say, a cellar; but this time, there was a great honor waiting for me, because with Sister Julienne and Sister Elisabeth, I am going to guard the Blessed Sacrament, which is kept there. Oh, my God, how good you are to stay with us! And how rich you make this poor niche seem when you honour it with your presence!

The parish priest wants to go to Ypres today and I will accompany him. He has gone on first in an ambulance car. The Countess van der Steen and I will follow by car, shortly.

12 MAY – Entering our beloved city, yesterday, a vague fear gripped us, everything is so bleak! I could not believe that I could live there for 27 weeks in the middle of ruins and rubble. We entered the convent, where we removed part of what remained of our church ornaments and those of Saint-Pierre and the Soeurs Noires. Whatever the cost, I also wanted to bring a pot of butter to celebrate my return to Poperinghe, but I was nearly never able to return from there, as when I left the cellar I was welcomed by a new salvo of bombing. Frightened, I banged the pot against a step of the stairs and found myself standing there, still holding the handle between my fingers! 'Come on! Quick!' they cried to me, 'Your pot might cost you your life!' We laughed a lot at my misadventure. Commander Young did not wish to expose the ladies to danger any longer, and I had to hasten to rejoin the Countess, whose car took us to Saint Augustine, to wait for the others, because the parish priest and some Friends continued in charge of the ambulance; they buried four corpses that had had to be left in plain view, two days ago. Halfway from Vlamertinghe, where we stopped, I had the pleasure of meeting Dr. Fox and Dr. Manning who were working there in an aid station erected in the St. Augustine Inn.

When the Sacré Coeur was hit, during the bombing of Ypres, a dressing station was maintained in the hospital to treat the many civilians wounded. When this was no longer viable, it was moved to an estaminet in Augustine Straat, a short distance along the Poperinghe Road. It was run by two FAU doctors and five orderlies and was also the base for five of the Unit's ambulances during this time. Amidst a constant chaos of shelling and bombing, wounded were rescued, treated at the dressing station, then taken on, if necessary, to the hospital in Poperinghe.

13 MAY – Feast of the Ascension! I helped a little in the hospital yesterday. At night, a dozen shells arrived, but it was child's play compared to what we were sent in Ypres. Today, I will accompany the parish priest to Saint-Omer to take the church ornaments and the figure of Our Lady of Thuyne.

14 MAY – The Directrice of the Saint-Denis boarding house, in Saint-Omer, who has already received Sister Josephine of the Soeurs Noires, several weeks ago, also offered me hospitality and, in addition, a bedroom, and an attic in which to keep the rescued items, as the parish priest intends to return to Ypres to carry on looking for anything of value. Everything will be packed in large crates and deposited in the allotted place.

JUNE – It is only today that I resume my journal: few or no incidents occurring since my stay at the Saint-Denis boarding house. What a contrast between the calm of the past few days with my eventful life during the long weeks in Ypres! Twice since I was in Saint-Omer, I returned to my home city . . . city! Does that term still suit this heap of ruins and rubble where so many beauties and riches are buried? During one of these quick visits, I entered the convent. Someone had made thorough searches in the cellar; all packages were opened and feather pillows split; undoubtedly, someone had hoped to find a hidden fortune.

The bottles of ink and sorrel had been thrown pell-mell. I made a brief inspection of the classrooms but the bombing was intense and I dared not prolong my visit, especially as I had a hand injury, which a *gendarme* helped me to dress. I was eager to return to Saint-Omer to unload the two ambulances that we had met.

In the meantime, my affairs concluded, I occupy myself in caring for residents.

26 JUNE – The parish priest came to announce my departure for England. Mr. G. W. Young, who has just returned from spending a

few days there, has met with Belgian families around his residence who would be happy to have among them Belgian Sisters to teach their children. He has proposed that the parish priest send me with a colleague. We will live with his parents; we will lack nothing in the religious respect; and, as the work will not be heavy, I will find some peace and the rest I need. The parish priest could not refuse and Sister Gérarde, designated to accompany me, will be notified by telegram.

Geoffrey Young was soon to leave Flanders for his family home of Formosa, Berkshire, where he would put the finishing touches to his plans to take out an ambulance unit to Italy. He arranged with Curé Delaere to take Soeur Marguerite, Soeur Gerarde and the Belgian Boy Scouts who had worked for them, for a holiday in England. The young nun could not conceal her obvious delight at the prospect.

14 JULY – I am back in Poperinghe. It will take some time before my colleague is in possession of the papers required to go to England, and typhoid fever being declared here, Mr. G. W. Young picked me up in Saint-Omer, to help in the new 'Search Party' he wants to organize.

My departure from Saint-Denis boarding house has made me very sensitive. During the six or seven weeks I was there, I formed a real affection for the ladies and residents of this establishment, of whom I will always keep the fondest memories and who are worthy of praise. The kindness and charity of which I have been the object have stirred in my heart the deepest gratitude.

16 JULY – We launched the 'Search Party' today. Our first searches are centred on Elverdinghe. I have to 'partner' Mr. Goodbody. Cases of typhoid are rare on this side, given the small number of inhabitants that remain. The houses we visit, one by one, are all empty; in cellars, the shoots on the potatoes, sometimes 50 centimetres high, form veritable green fields. The church is bombed and the cemetery battered.

17 JULY – Six cases of typhoid in Vlamertinghe.

18 JULY – I went this morning to visit Dean Debrouwer, among the Soeurs Paulines, installed in De Vogel. It is noteworthy that in most cases of typhoid fever, it is last year's typhoids that are the cause. This is why all those who were attacked by the disease should report to the doctors for careful examination.

19 JULY – Yesterday, in a house filled with British soldiers, located in woods between Vlamertinghe and Elverdinghe, we found a young girl dying of fever. She was taken to the St. Elizabeth hospital. We had visited 63 houses and, dead tired, we were preparing to stop work to go to the Farm Hospital, where we were to wait for the ambulance car, when there was an incident that I found quite pleasant.[39] We were sitting by the ditch in front of the farm, examining an artillery map, as it was used, today, to prepare the itinerary for our excursions. Suddenly a Taube came in reconnaissance.

The sentry at the door of the farm became suspicious, and, after exchanging a few words with a British policeman, he came right at us and, without saying a word, grabbed us by the collar! Mr. Goodbody was frightened. He asked for our papers, but he lacked any air of reassurance, and a soldier, bayonet fixed, was given the task guarding us. A farmer, passing by, did not hesitate to exclaim: 'Ah, ha! I have also thought that this nun and this officer were German spies!'

Meanwhile, upon a whistle given by the policeman, an officer presented himself and, without a word, examined us from head to foot. Two of our companions, Mr. Clibborn[40] and G. Thompson[41], passing at that moment, witnessed the scene, and were very much amused. But Mr. Goodbody did not appear to be amused by the adventure. As for myself, for whom it presented nothing new, I could not but approve of these brave soldiers, who, after all, were only fulfilling a grave duty. So many times their good faith was seen as betrayal, that we could not blame them for being wary even of the religious headdress.

After an hour and a half, a colonel, who knew from the report that was filed each evening at the military office, that the Quaker ambulance was currently serving the 6th Division, came to get us out of this mess and, after receiving suitable apologies, we got into the ambulance that arrived at that moment.

20 JULY – This morning, I went with Mr. Dunning[42] to look for typhoids. We found 14 in one house! All the girls had lost their hair, and it was quite strange to see them running about like that.

We lost our way in the woods! The English have made new roads with which we were not familiar. Furthermore, the networks of wire and trenches formed veritable mazes and although we could see in the distance the farm we had to reach, we were unable to get there. After two hours of searching, we were all happy to reach the edge of the woods and a familiar route.

Vlamertinghe was bombed for 3 hours. The damage will be quite extensive as 40 shells have already fallen.

21 JULY – Long live Belgium! This is the cry which still comes, today, from the heart of every child of the Fatherland, who, in their unhappiness, will be even more loved! I cannot believe that so much suffering, courage, endurance, heroism should not be in the right, against the brute force that would destroy us. God, justice and right-eousness, are they are not stronger than the material country? Belgium may suffer, agonize perhaps; die, never!

Colonel Trembloy will pick us up this morning from the deanery, at about 7 o'clock, to take us Ypres! It will be a worthy way to cele-brate this beautiful day! I will see my beloved hometown and my father's house. The one and the other have no more than ruins to offer me, but to see them again, it will give me renewed hope.

22 JULY – Sister Berchmans and 3 *Dames de Rousbrugge* also left yesterday! It is at the convent of the *Dames* that we have had lunch. The presence of a colonel again helped lead the conversation towards the war and the valiant heroes. How beautiful our soldiers are, with their unwavering bravery! How beautiful our King is, with his proud energy, in all the noble audacity of his heroic resistance!

Around 9 o'clock Search Party members were waiting at the St. Elizabeth Hospital. Lunch was eaten outdoors; we visited 40 fami-lies between Poperinghe and Proven.

23 JULY – I went back to Ypres yesterday. It was not in a nice car this time, but on a truck in the company of 22 travelling Belgian soldiers, and a *gendarme*. Pianos were taken to the *Dames de Rousebrugge* and while they were being loaded onto the truck, I went to take a look in the city. The parish priest and Sister Berchmans went before me in the first truck; but there was nobody in the neighbour-hood. I would have liked to take some of the books in my classroom to England, but the stairs leading up to it were completely destroyed. But, in wartime, one becomes ingenious. A plank helped me climb, with some difficulty, the pile of rocks which formed an obstacle, and I could take what I wanted. With my little treasures wrapped in my apron, I let myself slide along the plank and, fearing that they were already waiting for me, I hurried to the car. I left, giving the parish priest and Sister Berchmans the task of plundering the library of Monsieur Principal of the College. I arrived at the hospital in time to accompany Mr. Dunning on his visits to thirty small farms. There were hardly any patients there.

We returned, soaked, as we were surprised by a storm while waiting for the car that was to take us back to the hospital. At half past 6, Dr. Manning gave us an English lesson.

28 JULY – The Search Party completed its recent days in Proven, Elverdinghe, etc., wherever the 6th English division was stationed. We have most of our meals outdoors.

Yesterday I went to Ypres for the last time before I go to England, and this morning I returned to Saint-Omer to take the baggage that I still had. It gave me pleasure to see the good ladies and residents of Saint Denis who, in turn, seemed happy to see me, too.

At half past 9, Sister Gerarde arrived. I went to collect her from the station; we arrived in Poperinghe at midnight.

29 JULY – We packed our suitcases to go to England. This is a great event for us because we are leaving all our beloved community on this side of the sea. But for us, obedience comes above all else, and however great the sacrifice seems, we must resign ourselves to it.

30 JULY – The cannons, and, no doubt, also the emotions, have prevented us from sleeping. The priest went to Ypres this morning at 7 o'clock after he had bid us farewell and given us his last advice. It pains me to leave this good Father and to take the road to exile. May God guard us and sustain us there!

We waited for commander Young who would come to collect us at around 9 o'clock. These moments before the separation from my dear sisters were horribly painful for me. The 27 weeks spent together in the midst of danger, sharing the same anxieties and the same cares, have doubled our mutual affection and a vague premonition makes me fear that we shall not meet again in this world.

We leave today for Boulogne, where commander Young will lead us first to the Belgian Consulate to get our passports. If we can get our papers in time, we will take the boat this same evening.

31 JULY – We arrived in London yesterday evening at about half past 9. The crossing was quite good. The commander, who is always full of attention and kindness towards us, took us to his brother's house in Kensington Square where we spent the night.

This morning, Miss Nora, the Commander's niece, took us to see some of London's beauties, including the magnificent Westminster Cathedral.

This afternoon, she will take us to Cookham, to the home of Mr. Young's parents.

1 AUGUST – We are at 'Formosa' the patrimonial home of our great benefactor. Sir George and Lady Young were very pleased upon our arrival. We were touched by their warm welcome and their

attentive care. We found in them the truly paternal kindness that we had always been shown by the commandant.

11 AUGUST – In recent days, a Quaker camp has been organized here, that will then go on to Italy. Mr. Thompson, Barbour, Gray, Roose and Baker who we had met in Ypres, are part of the new ambulance. Everyone was subjected to anti-typhoid inoculations.

12 AUGUST – Last night, there were 5 patients in the camp, undoubtedly the result of the serum! Around 10 pm, I went to find them with Sir George who was holding a lamp in his hand. It was so dark that, whilst walking through the garden, where there was a pond, I thought, several times, that he would fall in. I held him by the jacket, waiting for the false step which, fortunately, did not transpire.

This morning, our sick were healed, thanks to the aspirin administered last night.

13 AUGUST – This morning, we provided new ropes and buttons for the officers' uniforms. The Duchess of Vendome, her daughter and her son, the Prince of Bourbon, with the Comtesse d'Ursel, came to Formosa to have tea and to see the camp.

14 AUGUST – The mansion is full. We are going to spend a week in Hurst, Cookham-Dene, at the home of Lady Young's sister.

17 AUGUST – The reception at the home of Mrs. Tuke and Miss Walrond was very cordial. These ladies lavish their attentions on us and cannot do enough to make our stay as pleasant as possible. We are occupied, with them, in making small bags of canvas which, filled with sand, will be used in the trenches.

18 AUGUST – We came back to Formosa, where there was a large gathering before the departure of the ambulance that will set sail, tomorrow, for Italy. The young volunteers were doing their practical exercises and dressings perfectly.

The Italian ambassador, who attended the party, made a speech in English.

19 AUGUST – Dr. Thompson, who plans to return to Poperinghe in a few days, came to visit us. We also received a visit from the reverend Father Curtin, parish priest of Maidenhead, and Miss Coleman, the great benefactress of the Catholic works in that town.

20 AUGUST – The ambulance cars were arranged in order, in the grounds of the château, waiting for the starting signal. Mr. G. W. Young left at about 11 o'clock. He was sorry to leave us.

Around 3 o'clock, Mrs. Tuke and Miss Walrond arrived to assist with the disbanding of the camp. Everyone filed past Sir George and Lady Young, offering thanks and showing great enthusiasm. The 'Hip, hip, hurray!' resounded on all sides, and, in turn, each came to share with us a good handshake which we accompanied with a: 'Good bye', and many best wishes, especially for those who had devoted themselves to us, and with us, in our dear city of Ypres!

2 SEPTEMBER – Here we are, after more than a month in the château 'Formosa' where we have passed happy and peaceful days. Here, no bombs or shells or shrapnel! This time of moral and physical rest has truly had a good influence on us. Under the gentle and loving concern of Sir George and Lady Young, we forget the bitterness of exile, not forgetting Miss Nora, who has also devoted herself to our happiness. However, because of the distance from a Catholic church, our stay here cannot be extended any longer.

4 SEPTEMBER – We have left 'Formosa' and its dear inhabitants, to come to 'Kenmora', where Miss Mary Coleman received us with unparalleled kindness. I would even say with appreciation. We expect that here, after September, we will be able to open a Belgian school in Maidenhead, for which Miss Coleman has taken it upon herself to assume any pecuniary costs. It is she who wants to be responsible for finding and paying for the necessary building, and all the necessary objects and equipment. Children who live a long way from the school will be given lunch there at noon, and rail tickets or passes will be procured for them.

5 OCTOBER – A few days ago, we opened our school in the 'Liberal Club'. A few children attend regularly, although some come from far away.

16 NOVEMBER – Four of our children have had the joy of having their first communion this morning. The ceremony was simple and touching. It would seem that, in exile, one appreciates even more the extent of divine favours.

21 NOVEMBER – On this day, Monsigneur W. Cotter, Bishop of Portsmouth, conferred the Sacrament of Confirmation on 13 of our children; we have taken advantage of the opportunity to let them

take their Holy Communion. Miss Coleman, whose generosity is inexhaustible, wanted to make the day a true feast for parents and children; she offered everyone a wonderful banquet. Everyone will keep a touching and indelible memory of this beautiful day. The only criticism that the good Miss Coleman deserves is that she spoils us too much, us and all the Belgians who are in Maidenhead. We can never repay her unfailing dedication. – The reverend Father Curtin is also a true father to our little Belgian colony. His kind words and his wise advice support us and comfort us, and we rely on him in all our difficulties.

With these two great benefactors, we also associate all members of the Committee for Belgian Relief. We will never forget all they do for us with wholehearted and continued selflessness. The memory of their good works will remain forever in our hearts and will make more fervent the prayers that are given up to God who has promised not to leave without reward, a glass of water given in his name. To all, yes all, our eternal gratitude!

Alas! My premonition on leaving Ypres has already been sadly fulfilled: our good Sister Berchmans is no more! We have just learned that she died in Poperinghe. The good God undoubtedly did not want to delay the reward that she had earned for her charitable devotion and courageous virtue! May she rest in peace!

Farewell, dear and good Sister! In crying, here, over your premature demise, I can but repeat to you these words, the last that we exchanged at the time of our separation: 'Farewell! Until Heaven!'

Here ends my diary: on 9 November 1916, I was recalled to Belgium, to fulfill another mission.

THE END

EPILOGUE

The 'other mission' to which Soeur Marguerite refers was no less than to take part in the rebuilding – both spiritual and material – of her beloved Ypres or, rather, of the vast and desolate expanse of mud and blackened débris that once had been Ypres. By the time Soeur Marguerite saw it again, after the war, the ruined town that she left had, incredibly, undergone further prolonged and relentless bombardment as the centre of further battle. Undefeated, Soeur Marguerite would throw herself with characteristic energy and enthusiasm, into playing what part she could in the gradual rebirth of the town.

While the town was rebuilt, under the watchful eye of Curé Dealere, now Dean of Ypres, the returning citizens were housed in temporary wooden shelters on the outskirts of the town. Here, Soeur Marguerite opened schools and helped untiringly in the innumerable tasks of renovation, before ill-health eventually forced her to retire to the peace and tranquility of her convent.[43]

The curé lived to see his cherished cathedral, the churches and convents, the Cloth Hall and other civic buildings rebuilt stone by stone, before he, too, retired to live in a large girls' orphanage that he had founded near Bruges, and where he died on 18 December 1936.

After the evacuation of Ypres, in 1915, the Friends' Ambulance Unit continued its work in the civilian and military hospitals it had established in Poperinghe and Dunkirk and created further facilities. It extended its ambulance work for the French Army, along almost the entire length of the Western Front, and staffed hospital ships and trains. After the Armistice the FAU continued to work in civilian relief and repatriation. It finally ceased to operate in 1919, but would be revived upon the outbreak of WWII.

Shortly after Italy entered the war, on the side of the Allies, Geoffrey Winthrop Young led the Anglo-Italian Ambulance Service out to the mountains around Gorizia, on the Italian–Austrian front. In Italy, as in Belgium, the ambulance unit volunteers earned an outstanding reputation. In August 1917 Young was hit by a shell and his left leg was so badly wounded that it had to be amputated at the knee. This did not curb his passion for mountaineering however, and, using an artificial leg, he continued to make important climbs, including that of the Matterhorn, in 1928. A strong interest in education eventually led Young to become a lecturer on Comparative Education at London University. He married, and he and his devoted wife, Eleanor, had a son and daughter.

Young visited his cherished friends on several occasions, and observed the reemergence of Ypres. His admiration for Soeur Marguerite deepened with the passing years:

> Soeur Marguerite had never been strong; but her spirit made her a leader again at once; through the years of rebuilding, and of recasting the life of the city. She wrote her remarkable *Journal d'une Soeur d'Ypres*; and then she withdrew from her years of adventure and her fame, and resumed with the same concentrated spirit her teaching and her little books and her pictures for the children ... Hers remains a life of consistent beauty: the beauty of heroic action, of an intrepid gaiety, and of a wonderful combination of the spiritual and the humorous visions of human existence.[44]

NOTES TO THE INTRODUCTION AND DIARY

1 The affluent town was subject to repeated enemy invasions.
2 The Ieperlee is the canalized river that that flows through the city of Ieper (Ypres), giving its name to the city. During the First World War, the river was part of the frontline. It linked the Ypres Salient, held by the French and English, to the Yser Front, held by the Belgian Army.
3 Jansenism was a Catholic theological movement, begun by Cornelius Jansen, primarily in France, that challenged Jesuit assumptions. It emphasized original sin, human depravity, the necessity of divine grace, and predestination. It was soon quashed, however, and religious conformity prevailed.
4 There were many religious orders and institutions in Flanders, including the Soeurs Grises, Soeurs Noires, Soeurs Clares Pauvres and Clares Riches.
5 The nuns of the Marie Convent were teachers in one of the several religious schools in the town.
6 The Cavalry School of the Belgian Army was in Ypres. Its barracks were near the Lille Gate, with an exercise area in Polygon Wood, a few miles to the east of the town.
7 *Marmite*, French term meaning 'cooking pot', was used to describe this particular kind of shell.
8 The 'casements' were the underground passageways and chambers forming part of the old defensive ramparts of the town. During the coming months, it was here, in airless, crowded and insanitary conditions, that thousands of Yprois took shelter from the bombardments.
9 The civil authorities of Ypres had now abandoned the town and the new Committee of Public Safety was formed in the cellars. It took charge of policing, street-clearing, fire-extinguishing and, when bombardment permitted, burying the dead.
10 Thomas Kerrinckx and Joseph Cottenier.
11 Frederick Harding had deserted from his unit and was later tried

and convicted of the offence, by the British Army. He served a prison sentence, but was saved from a worse fate by the intervention of the FAU members alongside whom he had worked, for several months, administering medical aid to the sick and wounded in Ypres.

12 The Friends suspected the ubiquitous Miss Cloostermans of being a spy.

13 This account appears almost verbatim in Geoffrey Winthrop Young, *The Grace of Forgetting* (London: Country Life Limited) 1953, pp. 195–196.

14 *Ibid.*

15 The Friends had established an emergency clinic in the St Marie Convent.

16 Geoffrey Young revealed that he and his men, undecided, at first, as to whether Mlle Cloostermans was spy or heroine, nicknamed her the 'speroine'!

17 See Geoffrey Winthrop Young, *The Grace of Forgetting* (London: Country Life Limited) 1953, pp. 198–199.

18 Feast of the Immaculate Conception of the Blessed Virgin Marie.

19 A large and well equipped military hospital established in the Grand Hôtel de l'Océan, on the coast at La Panne, by Royal surgeon Antoine Depage, in collaboration with the Red Cross. The Queen of Belgium was patron.

20 The Sacré Coeur was evacuated on 21 December, but would become operational again on 26 December. There had been quite extensive damage and many of the windows were broken, but no other suitable building could be found to house the hospital.

21 The Day of the Holy Innocents or 'Childermas' is in remembrance of Massacre of the Innocents – the biblical account of infanticide by Herod the Great, the Roman-appointed King of the Jews. According to the Gospel of Matthew, Herod ordered the execution of all young male children in the vicinity of Bethlehem, so as to avoid the loss of his throne to a newborn King of the Jews whose birth had been announced to him by the Magi.

22 The nuns enjoyed a Christmas party with the FAU. They joined in the laughter and singing, and marvelled at the kindness of the people in Britain who had sent food and other presents, to help bring some joy to their otherwise anxious and unhappy lives. Despite being amidst hardship and terrible suffering, Christmastime brought some happier moments.

23 Soeur Marguerite refers to the *Galette des Rois* – the French equivalent of the British Christmas cake, traditionally eaten on 6 January, during the festivities of the Day of the Three Kings.

24 These were the earliest typhoid cases reported.

25 After initial protest, the FAU doctors finally had to agree to allow typhoid cases into the hospital Sacré Coeur. Two isolation wards were opened to house them.

26 Letter signed: 'The Secretary, A. Vanhiemenhond, the President, A. Stoffel, Charles Delaère, Curé of St. Pierre', and dated Ypres, 23rd December 1914. Translation from French published in *The Friend*, 8 January 1915, pp. 22–23.

27 The British 2nd Army authorised the Friends' Ambulance Unit to put in place these measures to help combat the typhoid epidemic.

28 The sluice gates built into the town's defences had been opened to flood the surrounding plains, in an attempt to increase resistance to attack.

29 Medical student Kenneth Harry Tallerman served with FAU from 31 November 1914 to 13 October 1915. Medical student Donald Wallice served with the FAU from 2 February 1915 to 22 October 1915.

30 Tatham, Meaburn, and James E. Miles, *The Friends' Ambulance Unit 1914–1919: A record*, London: The Swarthmore Press Ltd., 1919.

31 There was a moat surrounding the town.

32 The Sacré Coeur hospital could no longer cope with the amount of typhoid cases being discovered and to help alleviate the strain, on 18 January, the FAU opened its second civil hospital, Château Elisabeth, in neighbouring Poperinghe.

33 Geoffrey Winthrop Young, *The Grace of Forgetting*, London: Country Life Ltd., 1953, p. 217.

34 In addition to food and clothing, many people in Britain donated assorted other items, including games and toys, for the deprived, sick and orphaned children.

35 A rochet is a white vestment generally worn by a Roman Catholic or Anglican bishop in choir dress. It is similar to a surplice, except that the sleeves are narrower. In the Roman Catholic tradition, the rochet comes below the knee and its sleeves and hem are sometimes made of lace. The 'velum' is the cowl.

36 This is a reference to the 42cm Howitzer gun hidden in Houthulst Forest to the north of the town. This enormous long-range gun was nicknamed 'Dicke Bertha' by the German Army – 'Big Bertha', to the British troops. From mid-April onwards, it was used in the deliberate and merciless bombardment of Ypres.

37 Lace-making was the major field of employment for Flemish women.

38 Medical card found among the FAU records for the Château Elisabeth Hospital, Poperinghe, held in the National Archives of Belgium, Brussels.

39 Prolonged bombing later prompted the FAU to move the Hospital Elisabeth to the nearby Ferme de Ryke, which became known as the 'Farm Hospital'. This did not take place until 22 August, however. It may be possible that the FAU was using a farm as an emergency station, at that point.

40 Musician Arnold Shewell Clibborn served with the FAU from 27 January 1915 to 1 May 1915.

41 Orderly Geoffrey Thompson served with the FAU from 27 January 1915 to 18 August 1915.

42 Insurance salesman Edwin Wilson Dunning served with the FAU from 5 January 1915 to 24 January 1919.

43 The two older boys went back to Ypres after a camping holiday on the Cornish coast. They eventually enlisted in the Belgian Army. Young arranged for the youngest, Maurice, to serve an apprenticeship as a motor mechanic, in England. After working with the ambulance unit in Italy, he returned to Ypres, where he did very well for himself.

44 Geoffrey Winthrop Young, *The Grace of Forgetting*, London: Country Life Limited, 1953, pp. 269–270.

Printed and bound by CPI Group (UK) Ltd, Croydon, CR0 4YY

13/04/2025

14656603-0004